MARRIAGE, DIVORCE,

&

REMARRIAGE

By

Charles J. Kriessman III, Ph.D.

Disclaimer

The author of this work has quoted the writers of many articles and books. This does not mean that the author endorses or recommends the works of others. If the author quotes someone, it does not mean that he agrees with all of the author's tenets, statements, concepts, or words, whether in the work quoted or any other work of the author. There has been no attempt to alter the meaning of the quotes; and therefore, some of the quotes are long in order to give the entire sense of the passage.

Copyright © 2015 by Dr. Charles J. Kriessman
All Rights Reserved
Printed in the United States of America

REL006201: Religion: Biblical Studies - Topical

ISBN: 978-0-9962591-5-6

All Scripture quotes are from the King James Bible except those verses compared and then the source is identified.

No part of this work may be reproduced without the expressed consent of the publisher, except for brief quotes, whether by electronic, photocopying, recording, or information storage and retrieval systems.

Address All Inquiries To:
THE OLD PATHS PUBLICATIONS, Inc.
142 Gold Flume Way
Cleveland, Georgia, U.S.A.

Web: www.theoldpathspublications.com
E-mail: TOP@theoldpathspublications.com

1.0

DEDICATION

This book is dedicated to my wife of twenty years, who has truly given her life for her family. She is truly the love of the author's life, who credits her with the fullness of God's love in raising our daughter. She has also proven invaluable as a mother and counselor to her three adult sons who love her dearly. She has been given extension of that love by God for her two grand-daughters who are very dear to her.

Her values and influence to her children and grandchildren only help to make this country stronger in a time of extreme delusion, rebellion, and chaos.

Dr. Charles Kriessman
July, 2015

TABLE OF CONTENTS

DEDICATION 3
TABLE OF CONTENTS 5
INTRODUCTION 9
    The Family 9
    Attacks on Marriage 11
    Our Present President 12
    What If? 13
    Many Views 14
    Four main views will be discussed: 15
    The Economics of Marriage 16
CHAPTER 1: MARRIAGE 23
    Ceremonial Considerations 24
    Necessity of Legality 27
    Marriage Development After Christ 29
    Roman Empire 30
    Germanic Kingdoms 31
    Consent 31
    Cohabitation 33
    Common-Law Marriage 34
    Clandestine Marriages 34
    Consanguinity 36
    Consummation 37
    Miscegenation (Mi-se-je-na-shen) 40
    Nazi-Germany 42
CHAPTER 2: WHAT IS A MARRIAGE? 47
    God and Israel 49
    Preparations 52
    Called to the Lamb's Supper 56
    Song of Songs 57
    King Solomon 59
    The Song 62
    CHAPTER 2 65

CHAPTER 3	70
CHAPTER 4	71
CHAPTER 5	74
CHAPTER 6	83
CHAPTER 7	88
CHAPTER 8	95

CHAPTER 3: THE JUDGMENT SEAT 103
- Matters of Mercy 103
- The Seat 105
- Standing Before Christ 107
- Good or Bad Works? 108
- Gold, Silver, and Precious Stones 109
- Crowns 111
- The Five Crowns 111
- The Crown of righteousness. 112
- The Crown of Glory. 112
- The Incorruptible Crown 113
- The Crown of Life 113
- The Crown of Rejoicing 114

CHAPTER 4: PORNEIA 115
- Fornication 117
- Adultery 120
- Porneia Mean Fornication? 123
- Hillel and Shammai 125
- The Men 126
- On Divorce 127
- Bill of Divorcement 129
- BETROTHAL 130

CHAPTER 5: PHYSICIANS OF NO VALUE 135
- Southern Shame 139
- Old Mores vs New Mores 139
- Gail Riplinger 142
- Lies and Deceit 147
- Who is Gail Riplinger? 148
- Waite Interview, 1995 151

TABLE OF CONTENTS

A Phone Call 157
Letters, Threats, More Lies 160
Peter S. Ruckman 163
Ruckman and Divorce 165
Second Divorce.. 166
In Light of God's Words 167
CHAPTER 6: DIVORCE AND REMARRIAGE 175
  Divorce 175
  The Early Church and Church Fathers............... 177
  Hermas.. 177
  Justin Martyr 179
  Tertullian.. 180
  To Rome 182
  Erasmus + Protestant Tradition 184
  Roman Catholic Interuptus............................. 185
  The Erasmian View... 187
  The Results 191
  Erasmain Camps.. 194
  Divorce Prohibited 196
  Clear Scriptures 197
  Exception clauses? 198
  Betrothal Redux... 200
  The Nature of John 8:41 202
  The Rule of Last Mention................................ 205
  Against Remarriage.. 208
  Some Reasons Not to Divorce and Remarry....... 210
CHAPTER 7: HOMOSEXUALITY & MARRIAGE 213
  Introduction... 213
  Activist Judges 215
  Sin Of Homosexuality 219
  A.I.D.S.. 224
  Sodomite Promiscuity 229
  Unlawful Marriages.. 232
  Jesus And Same-Sex Marriage 238
  Traditional Marriage Of a Man And a Woman... 240

END NOTES: **247**
    Introduction 247
    Chapter 1 247
    Chapter 2 248
    Chapter 3 248
    Chapter 4 249
    Chapter 5 250
    CHAPTER 6 252
    CHAPTER 7 253
BIBLIOGRAPHY **255**
    BOOKS 255
    ARTICLES 260
INDEX OF WORDS AND PHRASES **267**
ABOUT THE AUTHOR **273**

INTRODUCTION

Big changes are in store for the human race in the near future. The global elite are itchy and excited to direct human evolution from now to eternity. Human cells can be converted into programmable manufacturing entities.

Now, imagine a world in which every newborn baby immediately has a little capsule implanted under the armpit. Inside are monitors, tiny amounts of hormones, a wireless transmitter and a receiver.[1]

Engineers may soon program life itself, manufacture new body parts and make self-programmable, artificially intelligent robots.

The Family

The family is the basic foundation block of every nation or society. God's definition of that family traditionally is one man and one woman joined together by God into one unit.

> *"Therefore shall a man leave his father and his mother, and shall cleave unto his wife: and they shall be one flesh."* (Genesis 2:24).

The family establishes the home scene,

has the purpose of raising a family, working to pay taxes to maintain the guarantees of the U.S. Constitution to free speech and practice of religion and the pursuit of happiness.

The multitude of post-modern day philosophies that upset the moral order of the God-ordained family structure contributes to and eventually destroys the social order. The most vivid example of the destruction of the social order is given to us in Genesis 19:23-25. Sodom and Gomorrah were destroyed and wiped completely off the face of the earth. To this day their whereabouts are unknown. These two cities and their society were wholly given over to the sexual sin of homosexuality.

> *"Even as Sodom and Gomorrah, and the cities about them in like manner, giving themselves over to fornication, and going after strange flesh, are set forth for an example, suffering the vengeance of eternal fire."* (Jude 7)

> *"And turning the cities of Sodom and Gomorrah into ashes condemned them with an overthrow, making them an example unto those that after should live ungodly;"* (2 Peter 2:6)

It seems that our country takes no heed to what God has to say. Many live today in outright rebellion against the Creator. To say anything about what God calls sin brings out the pejorative of being homophobic. We have no reason to be afraid (phobic) of gays or their homosexuality. God has already destroyed their flaunting of His laws once, and it looks as if He will have to do it again. There is no fear of God in their souls and God will bring judgment for that. The only fear is to fall into the hands of an all-consuming God.

> *"It is a fearful thing to fall into the hands of the living God."* (Hebrew 10:31)

Attacks on Marriage

Today's society as a whole treats traditional marriage as a heresy. It has not always been that way. The family, as God instituted it, was respected and revered in our society. It was understood that a strong family was a building block to a strong community. Strong communities led to a strong society which made for a strong country.

Irresponsible and low-information voters have elected irresponsible and progressive leaders. Lack of jobs and respect for hard work has stirred unrest in our society, and the breakdown of the family has broken down moral and cultural boundaries.

> *"If it be possible, as much as lieth in you, live peaceably with all men."* (Romans 12:18)

Living peaceably as neighbors in a society and building strong traditional marriages is becoming a challenge in our present post-politically correct society. Fascist style tactics are being used against Christians and secular individuals voicing favor for traditional marriage.

Our Present President

Things are compounded by having President Barack Hussein Obama in charge.

It was wonderful to all to have the United States put into the office of the Presidency the first black. Well, he's half black, but it's all good. However, it is all well and good to have the first black and politically correct President if it weren't for some glaring facts. First of all, no one really noticed Obama's upbringing and influences that was all Socialist, if not outright Communist. These influences bear directly on the type of policies implemented in the last six years. To implement a Socialist agenda it takes a certain amount of coercion and chaos. We have seen that Obama and

INTRODUCTION

those around him thrive on this. We are told in the Bible to pray and give thanks to our rulers and those in Government in order:

> *"That we may lead a quiet and peaceable life in all godliness and honesty."* (1 Timothy 2:2b)

What If?

What if America turns Socialist? If the Church is oppressed by the Government in a severe way, can marriages survive and glorify God? As in other oppressive societies the Church, which will mostly be apostatized, would likely have to be sanctioned by the Government. Families would be closely monitored for any Biblical teaching or any growth spiritually. All will have to be approved by Big Government and Big Brother will be looking over everyone's shoulder. Chip implants will be controlling the masses. These would be not only for the expressed purpose of discovering diseases, but the applications of total mind control are endless. This is on top of divorce rates skyrocketing, gay marriage, political and cultural upheavals, and the picture for Godly-marriages and a strong society are dimming fast.

Thankfully, God has given us a guide for a Godly marriage and divorce as given in the Bible. This is what will be presented here and the attempt to clear up the intense confusion as regards the many views on divorce and remarriage.

Many Views

There are as many as six or seven different views on marriage, divorce, and remarriage floating around in the Church. There are variants of these views. It is not presumptuous to say that there is confusion abounding. The separate groups clinging to their particular stand may not be confused to what they believe, but as a whole it presents a Church that is in confusion.

> *"For God is not the author of confusion, but of peace, as in all churches of the saints."* (1 Corinthians 14:33)

> *"For where envying and strife is, there is confusion and every evil work."* (James 3:16)

The unquietness caused by strife with Church leaders as well as within Christian homes is ungodly and hurts God. It is time to heal the family by having Church leaders teach what our Lord Jesus Christ said about marriage and divorce.

INTRODUCTION

Four main views will be discussed:

1. No divorce and no remarriage.
2. Divorce, but no remarriage.
3. Divorce and remarriage for infidelity. (Shammai position).
4. Divorce and remarriage for any reason. (Hillel position).

In Jesus' day the Pharisees contended with about everything He taught about divorce and remarriage. They had the Jews conditioned to all the wrong things, only because it was worldly and made them feel good. The Pharisees, just like ministers of today, did not understand the nature of marriage, the meaning of "one flesh", and the Biblical Scriptures pertaining to marriage and divorce.

Some of the major passages we need to understand and exegete are Genesis 2:24, Leviticus 18:6-18, Deuteronomy 24: 103, Matthew 5:32, Matthew 19:3-12, Mark 10: 2-12, and Corinthians 7:12-16.

We need to understand the Biblical terms of fornication and adultery and what they meant then and what they mean now. Our understanding will depend on these definitions and all that Jesus said to us as Christians to be good parents, citizens, and Church members. Knowing the different shades of meaning and usage of the Hebrew and Greek words found in Greek and Hebrew dictionaries and lexicons is essential. English usage and definitions, even from the correct period in time are incomplete and inadequate but still useful to gain the whole picture.

We may never come to a complete consensus about marriage, divorce, or remarriage, but we must try. If what Jesus taught can be understood from the Scriptures, then that understanding must be applied to our marriages. To do otherwise would be sin. As one author has summed up: "whatever Christians do it will all end up at the Judgment Seat of Christ."

The writer admits to be an abecedarian on this subject. However, no matter the beginning level of learning, the Lord Jesus in fear is the beginning of knowledge and wisdom. Surrounded by volumes on the subject and looking to the author and finisher of our faith, the work begins.

The Economics of Marriage

Why is it that fewer and fewer people in the United States are getting married? One big reason is economics, money. America is transforming to a Socialist economy and one of its tolls is the rate of marriages. There are a lot more live-

INTRODUCTION

together relationships, an outgrowth of the permissive 60s and 70s.

Bowling Green University, in their study found that the marriage rate in the U.S. has fallen dramatically for the past 100 years. Since 1920, from a rate of 92.3 marriages per 1,000 unmarried women, the rate had fallen to 31.1 marriages per every 1,000 unmarried women in 1972. The rate has fallen off by 60% since 1970 alone!

These rates have changed the landscape of married households. In 1950, U.S. households were made up of 78% married couples. Today that number stands at 48%! The fundamental building block of society is crumbling. The fact is, the more money you have, the more likely you are to be married. Those rates will also decline as American becomes more and more Socialist.

The statistics do not bode well the future of marriage in our country and perhaps for all of Western Civilization. It is getting so bad that out of the 925 single women surveyed, 75% said they would have a problem dating someone without a job. Only 4% of respondents asked whether they would go out with an unemployed man answered "of course."[2]

This is shocking and woeful since jobs,

MARRIAGE, DIVORCE, & REMARRIAGE

good solid high paying jobs, are at a premium today. It is a toxic environment for jobs as businesses in America are being destroyed faster than they are being created. Adding to the problem, the Pew Research Center has found that younger Americans give a lower value to marriage than they once did. Having children is lower on the scale, as is seeing the necessity of children to have a mother and a father to grow up happy.

44% of those 18–29 years old now believe marriage to be obsolete. Society tells them they can have the benefits of being married without ever having to make the commitment. The sexual revolution continues and leaves in its wake countless broken hearts, shattered dreams, unintended pregnancies, some leading to abortion, and devastated families.

The picture does not get any brighter. The U.S. is a world leader—in sexually-transmitted diseases. The Centers for Disease Control estimates that about one-third of the entire population of the U.S. currently has a sexually-transmitted disease.[3]

Living together is now the New Marriage. According to the CDC, 74% of all 30-year-old women have lived with a partner

INTRODUCTION

before marriage and that 65% of all cohabitants that get married have lived together first.[4]

The myth is that living together first will provide the answer when it comes to finding that ideal partner for life in a successful marriage; only the facts prove the opposite is true. The divorce rate is higher for married couples that cohabitated first than those that do not.

That brings us to the point that for a long time now, when it comes to divorce America takes the prize. This country has had the highest divorce rate in the developed world.

Just over 60 years ago less than 1% of all women in the United States were divorced, whereas that number is 15% and probably higher today.[5] Money, cheating, and a problem staying committed to one person for an extended amount of time cause divorce. This breeds isolation, loneliness, and the bottom of the marriage rate dropping out. The household is smaller today.

100 years ago, 4.52 people were living in the average U.S household, but now the average household consists of 2.59 people.[6]

We have the highest percentage of

single-parent households on earth. Children need structure, strong homes, one from a mother and a father. This is not being provided today on a mass scale. With more than half of babies born out of wedlock, unheard of 100 years ago, the situation is desperate. There is no father in the household in the highest percentages ever seen. Women delay having children later and later today. The biggest reason for this is money, economics.

In the United States, three-quarters of people surveyed by Gallup in 2013 said the main reason they were not having more children was a lack of money or fear of the economy. The trend emerges that the growth in the pool of potential workers, ages 20-64 is dwindling which signals trouble ahead. The labor pool expanded with the generation of Baby Boomers, but they are retiring with not enough workers to replace them.[7]

There are fewer children being born at the wrong time when they are needed for the economic future of this country.

An aging, retiring population, without the young blood needed to keep the financial promises and commitments fulfilled are spelling trouble for all. Socialist, progressive policies will fill the vacuum as the institution

INTRODUCTION

of marriage is weakened and crippled.

So many attacks are coming at marriages, the bedrock of the Church, our Nation, and our whole civilization. Will the Church itself survive; will marriage survive as a holy and sacred God-created institution? Sin, apathy, apostasy, false teachers, false prophets, religion, professing Christians, homosexuality and more, promise to sink us. May God help us as we look at things pertaining to marriage, divorce, and remarriage. By connecting the dots it can be ascertained whether or not the mainstream Church will awaken or combine with the Harlot as the remnant watches it slide into total oblivion which will be the Tribulation.

> *"Behold, I stand at the door, and knock: if any man hear my voice, and open the door, I will come in to him, and will sup with him, and he with me."* (Revelation 3:20)

CHAPTER 1
MARRIAGE

"And Adam said, this is now bone of my bones, and flesh of my flesh: she shall be called woman, because she was taken out of man. Therefore, shall a man leave his father and his mother, and shall cleave unto his wife: and they shall be one flesh." (Genesis 2:23, 24).

It seems that in today's post-modern, post-Christian society the culture's memory of traditional Biblical marriage is fading rapidly. Genesis 2:23, 24 marks the first mention of the first institution of Jehovah God. The bringing together of one man and one woman as one flesh, and blessing that union with one or several natural or adopted children was God's main intention for mankind.

God first formed a man from the dust of the elements of the Earth and breathed into him a spirit of life. God then formed a woman from a rib of Adam. Thus "...now bone of my bones, and flesh of my flesh." Marriage was instituted between the first man and the first woman before sin entered into the garden. After the fall of the first parents they settled into forming a family unit beginning with Cain and Abel. The institution of marriage created between one man and one woman founded the first family as the stable home environment in which to raise children. This was all God's will.

Ceremonial Considerations

Although God performed the first marriage ceremony in the garden (Genesis 2:24) this does not seem to satisfy some today. They complain that a ceremonial practice is not Biblical and consummation is all that is necessary for a marriage to be legitimate in God's eyes. No disrespect intended but such brummagem is not very becoming. More in depth evaluation of this and some of these combatants will follow later.

Of course the Bible does not give clear instructions on how to conduct wedding ceremonies. The marriages, feasts, and marriage customs in the Bible are based on cultural considerations at the time and throughout the Jewish and Gentile history. These were not commanded by God, but Scripture contains principles that serve to be helpful. These cannot be overlooked, minimized, or mocked since they collectively make up the will of God for the marriage institution.

CHAPTER 1: MARRIAGE

In ancient times Jewish historical marriage was very much a family affair. There are examples of families arranging marriages in the Old Testament in Genesis 24. Abraham pulled aside his main servant, when he was old, and commanded the servant:

> *"And I will make thee swear by the LORD, the God of heaven, and the God of earth, that thou shalt not take a wife unto my son of the daughters of the Canaanites, among whom I dwell:*
>
> *But thou shalt go unto my country, and my kindred, and take a wife unto my son Isaac." (Genesis 24: 3.4)*

Back then the bride would agree to live near the groom's family and not the other way around. The would-be bride's family would consent to all the arrangements. A gift would be given to the bride and her family to seal the agreement. An exception to this would be that Jacob and Esau chose their own wives. Esau took two wives, Judith a Hittite and Bashemath another Hittite. "Which were a grief of mind unto Isaac and Rebekah." (Genesis 26:35). Isaac also took two wives; Leah and Rachel. Thus we see the idea of polygamy practiced through Jacob and Esau. Polygamy was first introduced by Lamech, who "took unto him two wives." (Genesis 4:19) After the Jews had formed the habit, contrary to their moral customs and laws, of intermarrying with foreigners, they indulged in polygamy unrestrainedly. The captivity seemed to have stamped out this custom, however, for there is no instance or record in the Old Testament of its practice after the return from Babylon.

Choosing one's own spouse became the normal procedure. Now in Jewish custom a dowry is to be paid to the bride's family if the husband divorces the wife. There was much divorce in Jesus' time and that led to the Pharisee's hard questions to our Lord on marriage and divorce. Of course, there is a question whether or not the Christian actually chooses his spouse or if God does the choosing. What God does forms the foundation of marriage. This is what's needed to get back to today: allowing God to provide a man with a wife.

> "And the Lord God said, it is not good that the man should be alone; I will make him an help meet for him." (Genesis 2:18)

> "And the rib, which the lord God had taken from man, made he a woman, and brought her unto the Man." (Genesis 2:22)

The foundation of marriage is God bringing the woman to Adam as an help meet (helper) and a completion of the man. She

CHAPTER 1: MARRIAGE

was to complete Adam as a man and he was to complete Eve as a woman. Adam could not live without Eve and Eve could not live without Adam. A companion for Adam could not be found in the animal kingdom nor in the angelic world above. When a man or a woman do not prove to be a helper to each other, then that marriage is in trouble. When the man and the woman complement each other God is blessing in that marriage. The saying, behind every good man is a good woman, may be dated but it is still very true.

Necessity of Legality

Weddings should be a time of joy. The choosing of a bride and a groom has been made and it is time to get married and proceed into the marriage. Wedding ceremonies have not changed all that much up to this day. Many object to even the simplest ceremony to be married. What it should be is God honoring and sacred to each party. It should be between a man and a woman, just as God instituted it from the beginning.

> *"Have ye not read, that he which made them at the beginning made them male and female."* (Matthew 19:4)

A marriage must now be recorded and registered by the state. We must follow state

MARRIAGE, DIVORCE, & REMARRIAGE

laws and get marriage licenses, have the wedding officiated and signed off, and receive the marriage certificate. That is the law of the land and the reality is that we must obey the law. We honor God and his law when we do this and anything less is sacrilegious and an affront to our Lord.

Yes there are marriage laws in the United States, and many of our young either were never taught that fact or they want to ignore it as being obsolete and something relative to their beliefs. That is, leave us to our own devices so that we can do whatever we want.

If you are a minister you will be familiar with the marriage laws in your state. You may need to file credentials of ordination, or procure a license from your county or state to do weddings. You would need to know the amount of time you have after performing the wedding to return the marriage license to the county. All information needs to be done in accordance with county and state laws and any other requirements that need to be fulfilled.

For example, in the State of Arizona:

> Marriage can be performed by all regularly licensed or ordained clergymen.
>
> The license must be filed within 30

CHAPTER 1: MARRIAGE

days. You would need to contact the Clerk of the Superior Court for any questions.

In California:

The marriage can be performed by any minister, priest, or rabbi of any denomination of age of 18 years or older. The license must be filed within 4 days. Contact County Clerk with any questions.

In Illinois:

The marriage can be performed by clergy from any denomination or Indian Nation or tribe. The license must be filed within 10 days. Questions can be directed to the County Clerk.[1]

"Congress shall make no law respective an establishment of religion, or prohibiting the free exercise thereof;..."

Part of 1st Amendment

"...nor shall any State deprive any person of life, liberty, or property, without due process of law;..."

Part of 14th Amendment.

Our religious freedom is granted and guaranteed by the provisions of the Constitution, the Bill of Rights.[2]

Marriage Development After Christ

Having mentioned ancient Jewish traditions in marriage, the same kind of arrangements held pretty close to that up until the time of Christ. These involved a three-stage ritual. The Ketubbah would be the bride and groom agreeing to marry and the father of the soon-to-be bride signing the Ketubbah Contract. The Chuppah would be the final payment for the bride and the date setting for the sexual consummation of the couple. After the consummation a wedding feast would be held at the house of the groom. This ancient ritual is seen in some form from the time of Abraham to the first century.

Roman Empire

Marriage on the Gentile side took the form of a social and legal union between a man and a woman. There was some recognition by the governments and empires but this evolved slowly. In the Roman Empire marriage was a private arrangement between heads of households, typically of the same social class.[3]

There was no formal wedding ceremony. Dowries and gifts were exchanged thereby in theory publicly showing consent between the parties. Roman law included the importance of the honor of marriage shown by the husband's level of care for his wife. That together with

CHAPTER 1: MARRIAGE

his outward affection bonded the marriage, whereas the lack of one of these outward signs from the husband terminated the marital union.

Germanic Kingdoms

For the Germanic people marriage was a joining of a man and a woman and a union of the two created after cohabitation and consummation. There was polygamy, for it was not outlawed. They had marriage by kidnapping and rape, by the purchase of a wife, and marriage by mutual consent. In the second form there was a negotiated compensation for the bride's family. The power over the bride was transferred to the husband. The third form, consent, was given by the bride to the husband, no power was transferred from the bride to the husband, and the woman remained within the legal jurisdiction of her own family despite living with her husband. [4]

Since the three C's were first mentioned altogether in the Germanic Kingdom it may do well to define each: Cohabitation, Consummation, and Consent.

Consent

Consent has been theorized, debated, and written about by scholars for a very long time. To consent is to give permission or reach agreement for some activity to occur.[5] The type of consent needs to be understood as there are two kinds, originating and permissive. Permissive consent acts as a waiver to something that could be perceived as invasive or wrong but is considered not to be. An example would be to permit your dentist to drill out a cavity and not have it be considered invasive battery.

The type of consent we are most interested in would be originating. That is consent that is: introducing, altering and endorsing parts of this background itself.[6] One of the earliest examples of originating consent would be the Mosaic Covenant in which the Israelites consented to and affirmed divine authority upon their agreement. This consent on the part of the Israelites was given and a new fact of the relationship with Jehovah was enjoined.

In the 11th thru 13th centuries, or the Middle Ages, consent was the main catalyst for marriage. The Papal authorities used words in the present tense for the man and woman to consent to be married. This progressed to the more accepted notion of family consent that was prevalent during feudal times. Thus more individual responsibility was assumed and consent the

CHAPTER 1: MARRIAGE

legal motion necessary to legitimize marriage began to take root.

Cohabitation

Clearly there was non-Christian marriage before Christ. But there were forms of cohabitation with certain foundational qualities of Christian marriages of later periods. These included fidelity, exclusivity, and publicly proclaimed covenants of monogamy and faithfulness between partners. What was missing was God in the relationship, or any knowledge of God.

A promiscuous relationship of cohabitation may display outward signs of a true marriage. However, it is still promiscuous, based on mutual consent was given a modicum of dignity found in marriage, but it is still wrong in God's eyes. Cohabitation is not favorable to the Christian for several reasons. We could call those consenting to cohabitation and equating it to God-approved marriage as fornicators. We know that fornicators will not be in the Kingdom of God (Hebrews 13.4). Cohabitation is outside the boundaries of what God accepts as marriage. Fellow believers have entered into the same Church orientated and Godly covenants of marriage.

Christians exercise their duty to God by upholding the law as Romans 13 teaches, legally committing to the marriage laws of the state in which one resides.

Common-Law Marriage

Cohabitation moved on from pre-modern times to be renamed and given secular dignity as common-law marriage. This system originates from the Common Law of the English and American legal circles. Both partners in the relationship agree or consent to its own validity in this sui juris marriage. Usually these unions are not formally registered with either church or state. There are variations of relationships and benefits derived from common law. There are contracts of common law recognized in some places. A general rule is that common law marriages are not recognized as marriages, but for tax purposes and financial claims they are treated as if they were. These can be dangerous unions for a couple since they are liable to palimony laws which can be so individually devastating. Not an ideal situation, especially for Christians.

Clandestine Marriages

Consent for marriage was a problem

CHAPTER 1: MARRIAGE

for the State and for Catholic churches. They could not control nor regulate couples who go public with their consent to marry. This added continually to the practice of clandestine marriages through the 1750's. London, England was especially scandalized by this practice. People, according to released memoirs, had used the system of clandestine marriage to contract bigamous marriages in order to be protected from creditors.[7] The system was so abused it spawned the infamous and corrupt Fleet Street Marriage Markets.

Clandestine marriages were legally binding unions in which the couple had not completely followed the rules set by Canon Law. The Anglican Church required that the prospective union be announced by either the posting of banns (public marriage announcement) for three weeks before the intended ceremony or the issuance of a marriage license. The ceremony itself had to take place within the parish of one of the candidates between the hours of 8:00am and noon and abide by the service listed in the Book of Common Prayer.[8] These clandestine marriages were usually officiated by clergymen who were not in official capacity. They were most likely done in parishes not of the couple, and in places such as taverns, prisons, or even brothels.

These ceremonies were difficult to regulate, so much so that a seamy subculture engulfed clandestine marriage causing the Church to push back.

London's Fleet marriages caused the most stir, as they made a mockery of the law. In a several block area around the Fleet Street Prison, debtor clergymen who were incarcerated there were allowed to perform clandestine weddings. Fraud was rampant at the Fleet Street marriage houses. The Fleet marriages proved popular and very lucrative for the clergymen. They did provide the benefits of more legalized unions among lower class people, lower illegitimacy rates, and lighter parish burdens. Clandestine marriage was reformed under Lord Chancellor Hardwicke's Marriage Act of 1753.

Consanguinity

An important consideration when it comes to marriage is the blood relation of the man and the woman. We all have ancestors and we all have descended from them. The laws dictate degrees of consanguinity and these relate to prohibited sexual relations and intestate succession of property.

Usually if any question arises about blood relations a table showing lineal consanguinity is used. Incestuous

CHAPTER 1: MARRIAGE

relationships are to be screened out and marriage prohibited between them.

Consanguinity, therefore, affected two main things legally. It determined whether two people could marry. If relationships fell within the bounds of incest they were not permitted to marry. Here in the U.S. first cousins are forbidden to marry, as are siblings, half-siblings, aunts and uncles. In Roman Civil Law, later followed by the Catholic Church, couples were forbidden to marry if they were within four degrees of consanguinity, (blood ancestors.).

The second most relevant issue involved inheritance. If a person dies without a will the succession of inheritance follows the Uniform Probate Code of the United States Section 2-103.[9]

Consummation

We come at last to our final historical stop of the evolution of marriage which is consummation. Even though we traced consummation back to Germanic Kingdom times, its significance took on a larger meaning later in time. Consummation or consummation of a marriage, in many traditions and statutes of civil or religious law, is the first (or first officially credited) act of sexual intercourse between two people following their marriage to each other.[10]

Webster's says that to consummate is to make perfect; to make the marital union complete by sexual intercourse. So consummation is the act of consummating a contract by mutual signature: the consummating of a marriage. According to God and the Bible we are not made complete, as Christians, by a response or act (such as intercourse) that terminates a period of some goal-directed behavior. We are complete in Him and made perfect by His word.

> *And ye are complete in him, which is the head of all principality and power:"* (Colossians 2:10)

> *"All scripture is given by inspiration of God, and is profitable for doctrine, for reproof, for correction, for instruction in righteousness: that the man of God may be perfect, thoroughly furnished unto all good works."* (II Timothy 3:16, 17)

We do not need an act of consummation in a marriage to make ourselves or that marriage complete, though there are many today who feel we do. There will be more on that later. The legal significance of consummation relating to theories of marriage is at least four-fold. One purpose was for producing offspring as descendants according to law. It also

CHAPTER 1: MARRIAGE

provided sanctioning to a couple's sexual acts together. Consummation treats the marriage ceremony as not being enough to complete the creation of the state of being married. Hence, in a few Western World traditions marriage is not considered binding unless it has been consummated by a sexual act. There are all sorts of variants about consummation, including the English version of the royals being publicly witnessed in the act of consummating the marriage.

Before leaving the subject of consummation, maybe it would serve to try to understand:

> *"And they twain shall be one flesh: so then they are no more twain, but one flesh."* (Mark 10:8)

This will be fleshed out (no pun intended) later, but suffice it to say that marriage would not be necessary if only a sex act made two people married. We see in the Old Testament that if a man had unlawful sex with a woman, then he would be expected to marry her through all the necessary steps. If sex did make them married then the marriage ritual would be superfluous. If the total of sex partners in any of our lives constituted marriages, how many would each of us have? Why would the Lord God need to count and judge fornication and adultery as sin?

If becoming one flesh refers only to the sex act between two people, then the words of God, "therefore what God has joined together, let no man put asunder" (Mark 10:9) needs much more understanding and it will be dealt with in more detail.

One last note: With the advancement of Canon Law, the opposing forces of consent and consummation came to a head. The 12th Century Bolognese Master, Gratian, in his *Decretum*, a type of legal textbook, proposed that the formation of marriage was a two-stage process with consent between two individuals followed by the sexual consummation of marriage transformed marriage into a sacrament.[11]

Miscegenation (Mi-se-je-na-shen)

Webster defines miscegenation as sexual relations or marriage between people of two different races (such as a white person and a black person). The word comes from the Latin *miscere,* to mix and *genus,* race. A mixture of races; especially through marriage, cohabitation, or sexual intercourse between a white person and a member of another race.[12]

Popularly known as race-mixing, the

CHAPTER 1: MARRIAGE

term is used less frequently today in our politically correct society.

Miscenation: The Theory of the Races, Applied to the White man and Negro was a propaganda pamphlet printed in New York City in December of 1863, and is the first known use of the word.[13] The propaganda amounted to pushing the inter-marrying of white and blacks until the races were so totally blended as to be indistinguishable. It was also falsely claimed to be the goal of Republicans, when it was discovered to have been written by two Democrats seeking to discredit Republicans, Lincoln, and the abolitionist movement.

Miscegenation is widely reviled across the world, because it leads to the annihilation of racial integrity and a coalescing of different racial stocks which destroys radial diversity. Anti-miscegenation laws sprang up in all 13 original colonies from the late seventeenth century and also in many U.S. states and territories until 1967. This shows to what extent racial diversity existed in the U.S. and the efforts put forth to preserve that diversity and integrity. Opposition to mass-miscegenation came not only from whites but from every racial group. Black and Hispanic women complained that white women stole their men. Oriental men complained that white men would steal their women and so on.

Nazi-Germany

The Nazis discriminated against miscegenation in an anti-semantic way. The Protection of German Blood and German Honor Act of 1935 made marriage or extramarital relations between Aryans (persons of German or related blood) and non-Aryans illegal. This was extended to Gypsies, Negroes, or their bastard offspring. Never mind that there was no scientific or accepted Aryan race to begin with. That was a figment of Nazi racism.

There were approximately 20,454 so-called mixed marriages in Germany in 1939. Divorce between the couples was encouraged. It is said that none of the non-Aryan (Jewish) members of the marriages were deported or shipped off to concentration camps. However, upon the death of an Aryan spouse, the non-Aryan half was subject to persecution and shipped to the camps.

The children of the mixed marriages in Nazi Germany were called Mischling and were subject to discrimination. In March of 1943, the Germans attempted to deport Belin-based Jews and Gentiles of Jewish

CHAPTER 1: MARRIAGE

descent living in non-privileged marriages. A non-privileged marriage was classified as a wife being an Aryan and the husband being a Jew. This attempt was the only case in all of Nazi Germany that failed in deportation due to a public riot and protest by their relatives-in-law of Aryan kinship. This is documented in the book, *Resistance of the Heart.* When Nazi Germany was defeated in 1945 the anti-miscegenation laws were repealed. All restricted unmarried couples from the time were married and backdated to be recognized to legitimize children and sort out inheritances.

Miscegenation is a problem today in the Church. God has dealt with this issue, laying down a principle in the Old Testament. The line of Shem, which made up the Semites or Jews, was not to intermarry and bear children with the line of Ham or any other line, period. The line of Ham in Canaan included the Hittites, the Girgashites, the Amorites, and Canaanites, the Perizzites, and Hivites, and the Jebusites (Deuteronomy 7:1). If they did marry into Ham's line God predicted that they would be turned away from following Him, serve other gods in idolatry, bring the anger of God down on them, and cause God to destroy them. (Deuteronomy 7:4). The Egyptians, Ammonites, and Moabites were also not to be intermarried with. The Ammonites and Moabites were from the loins of Lot, Abraham's nephew. The Edomites were also forbidden to the Israelites.

The principle carried over to grass,

> "... the herb yielding seed, and the fruit tree after his kind, ..."(Genesis 1:11).

The grasses and herbs and fruit trees were to be pure and not mingled. The same was true for animals and fowls. "And God created great whales, and every living creature that moveth, which the waters brought forth abundantly, after their kind, and every winged fowl after his kind: and God saw that it was good." (Genesis 1:21). God did not allow His people to mix their seeds because of the danger of defilement. The seeds were equal to each other, just not to be mixed, the races were not to be mixed according to God and He made this very clear.

The Church's problem is that there is no knowledge of the issue.

> "My people are destroyed for lack of knowledge: because thou hast rejected knowledge, I will also reject thee, ..." (Hosea 4:6a)

As a post-modern, post-Christian

CHAPTER 1: MARRIAGE

Church, it may well be rejected as knowledge and the will of God on the way to Apostasy. It gets to the point where the Church leaders themselves are committing the trespass against God. As a result of this compromise the leaders should be warning the flock but that is not happening. The Church should not be bringing a curse of God upon it and appear to be compromising or going along with the world.

> *"For I have not shunned to declare unto you all the counsel of God." (Acts 20:27)*

Leaders and Pastors of the Church must follow the example that is in the Word of God.

CHAPTER 2

WHAT IS A MARRIAGE?

How did God intend marriage to be? Is there another application from God to the Christian couple? We know that the first marriage occurred in paradise.

> *"And the LORD said, it is not good that the man should be alone; I will make him an help meet for him."* (Genesis 2:18)

God made Adam a help meet as his wife and her name was Eve. He thus instituted marriage between a man and a woman and they were to help each other and complete each other.

> *"Therefore shall a man leave his father and his mother, and shall cleave unto his wife: and they shall be one flesh."* (Genesis 2:24)

Jesus Christ, when he was on the earth, confirmed marriage as being right and His will.

> *"And he said, for this cause shall a man leave father and mother, and shall cleave to his wife: and they twain shall be one flesh?*
>
> *Wherefore they are no more twain, but*

> one flesh. What therefore God hath joined together, let not man put asunder." (Matthew 19: 5, 6)

Webster tells us that marriage or wedlock is the institution whereby men and women are joined in a special kind of social and legal dependence for the purpose of founding and maintaining a family.

> "Because the Lord hath been a witness between thee and the wife of thy youth, against whom thou hast dealt treacherously; yet is she thy companion, and the wife of thy covenant." (Malachi 2:14)

Marriage is the solemn and sacred covenant that is entered into by the bride and groom before God and man. The Lord warns three times in three verses, (Malachi 2:13-15) not to deal treacherously with the wife of one's youth. God has made the two one, blessed them and the marriage and yearns for godly seed. (Malachi 2:15). The word treacherously comes from the Hebrew word *baghad*. It means to act covertly or fraudulently, secretly, deceptively; to cheat, betray, to oppress, to afflict, to spoil. All these things God repeatedly tells us to take heed against. We know the world does not care if it acts in this way, but must Christians turn their backs on God and go against the once sacred covenant? The Lord has joined

CHAPTER 2: WHAT IS MARRIAGE?

two into one in body and spirit and he hates the putting away of spouses today.

The act of God of putting the married man and the married woman together (Matthew 19: 5, 6) is a spiritual as well as a physical joining in wedlock. This is not done merely by a sexually intimate act only. "What, know ye not that he which is joined to an harlot is one body? For two, saith he, shall be one flesh." (1 Corinthians 6:16). God says nowhere in the Bible that this type of union is in any way, shape, or form equal to a marriage.

God and Israel

Marriage was a figurative way in which Jehovah God described his relationship with his people, the nation of Israel.

> *"For thy Maker is thine husband, the LORD of hosts in his name;"* (Isaiah 54:5a)

> *"And as the bridegroom rejoiceth over the bride, so shall thy God rejoice over thee."* (Isaiah 62:5b)

> *"Turn, O backsliding children, saith the LORD; for I am married unto you: and I will take you one of a city, and two of a family, and I will bring you to Zion:"* (Jeremiah 3:14)

So, in the Old Testament the Lord willingly took Israel to be His wife only to be rejected by Israel. They rejected His word, His law and turned to idols and other gods. She became adulterous and was abandoned as a wife. She will later be the wife restored.

> *"For the LORD hath called thee as a woman forsaken and grieved in spirit."* (Isaiah 54:6a)

> *"For a small moment have I forsaken thee; but with great mercies will I gather thee."* (Isaiah 54:7)

But Israel is not the Bride which is the Church. Backsliding Israel played the harlot in the day of King Josiah when God called out to her to no avail. She is not the virgin she was and therefore cannot be Christ's chaste bride. However, Israel will be a wife again and converted and He shall be her redeemer. Israel will be excellent and God will manifest Himself as the God of Israel and will appear as the God of the whole earth. Israel will no more be labeled forsaken (Isaiah 62:4), but she will be called Hephzibah (2 Kings 21:1) who was Hezekiah's wife, a type of Jerusalem, as Hezekiah was a type of the Messiah. Israel's land will be called Beulah, she will be the delight of God, married in the land with God's protection as well as His ownership. The nation and people of Israel

CHAPTER 2: WHAT IS MARRIAGE?

will be the earthly bride, separated for a time from her divine husband, but then reunited and restored to be the mother Church of the millennial earth.

> *"And to her (the Bride; the Church) was granted that she should be arrayed in fine linen, clean and white: for the fine linen is the righteousness of saints. And he saith unto me, blessed are they which are called unto the marriage supper of the Lamb."* (Revelation 19: 8, 9)

The Bride of Christ is the Church. All genuine, born-again believers in the Lord Jesus Christ make up the Church of Jesus Christ. The Bride of Christ is a virgin that the Lamb of God, which is Christ, is to marry. All those who were saved and taken out for a people, from Pentecost to the Rapture are Christ's betrothed Bride.

> *"Simeon hath declared how God at the first did visit the Gentiles, to take out of them a people for his name."* (Acts 15:14).

The Gentiles have been taken from a low estate of men, forgiven by the shed blood of Christ on Calvary and prepared as Christ's chaste Bride.

> *"Let us be glad and rejoice, and give honor to him: for the marriage of the Lamb is come, and his wife hath made*

herself ready." (Revelation 19:7)

That is, the raptured Church, the heavenly Bride, is soon to be transformed at His coming and be joined in marriage in perfect union with Christ personally and in His holiness, joy, and glory.

> *"Be glad in the Lord, and rejoice, ye righteous: and shout for joy, all ye that are upright in heart."* (Psalm 32:11)

> *"But let the righteous be glad; let them rejoice before God: yea let them exceedingly rejoice."* (Psalm 68:3)

Preparations

We have been joined to our Lord Jesus Christ spiritually and our relationship as the Church to Him as His betrothed Bride is spiritually symbolic.

> *"For we are members of his body, of his flesh, and of his bones. For this cause shall a man leave his father and mother, and shall be joined unto his wife, and they two shall be one flesh. This is a great mystery: but I speak concerning Christ and the Church."* (Ephesians 5: 30-32)

Paul represented his glorious relationship of the entire body of believers as the Church, to our Lord Jesus Christ thus:

CHAPTER 2: WHAT IS MARRIAGE?

> *"Husbands, love your wives, even as Christ also loved the church, and gave himself of it; that he might sanctify and cleanse it with the washing of water by the word, that he might present it to himself to a glorious church, not having spot, or wrinkle, or any such thing; but that it should be holy and without blemish."* (Ephesians 5: 25- 27)

We have another picture of what Christ is doing for His Bride and how he expects to receive her.

> *"For I am jealous over you with godly jealousy: for I have espoused you to one husband, that I may present you as a chaste virgin to Christ."* (2 Corinthians 11:2)

Christ is the Bridegroom

> *", he hath covered me with the robe of righteousness, as a bridegroom decketh himself with ornaments, and as a bride adorneth herself with her jewels."* (Isaiah 61:10B)

> *"And Jesus said unto them, can the children of the bridechamber mourn, as long as the bridegroom is with them?"* (Matthew 9:15a)

The presentation of the Church as the Bride without spot or wrinkle refers to a double fulfillment of Christ's work and the work done in the Church.

MARRIAGE, DIVORCE, & REMARRIAGE

> *"For the marriage of the Lamb is come, and his wife hath made herself ready."* (Revelation 19:7b)

All is made ready for the marriage of the Lamb and His Bride. Christ has prepared the way, all the way from Calvary's salvation, to providing grace for sanctification, to the vanquishing of His enemies to the judgment seat. The Spirit has worked in His Church, cleansing and making holy. The Bride of Jesus Christ has allowed the Spirit to drive the Church to live holy and clean lives. The Church has served the Lord in gladness, and received blessings in trial and tribulations.

> *"Blessed are ye, when men shall revile you, and persecute you, and shall say all manner of evil against you falsely, for my sake, rejoice and be exceeding glad: for great is your reward in heaven:"* (Matthew 5: 11-12)

For this sanctifying and coming through trials of fire,

> *"...to her was granted that she should be arrayed in fine linen, clean and white: for the fine linen is the righteousness of saints."* (Revelation 19:8)

The Bride will be clothed in fine, clean linen. White is the color of the purity of the Bride. The saved, born-again ones will have new bodies and have clothes of fine, white

CHAPTER 2: WHAT IS MARRIAGE?

linen. The righteousness of the saints is plural and denotes righteousness or righteous deeds.

Since the Lord Jesus Christ has died for our sins we should live unto righteousness. We do this by faith.

> *"And he believed in the LORD; and he counted it to him for righteousness."* (Genesis 15:6)

From very early on, from Abraham, faith has equaled righteousness in the words of God.

> *"But now the righteousness of God without the law is manifested, being witnessed by the law and the prophets; Even the righteousness of God which is by faith of Jesus Christ unto all and upon all them that believe:"* (Romans 3: 21-22)

Faith is unto all, but upon all them that believe. Those that genuinely trust in the Lord Jesus Christ have the righteousness of God. In trusting God and trusting Jesus Christ as Saviour and Redeemer we received God's righteousness, which we do not deserve. Faith in the Lord Jesus Christ equals righteousness in God's eyes. He gives us righteousness. We must follow after righteousness.

> *"For the grace of God that bringeth*

> *salvation hath appeared to all men, teaching us that, denying ungodliness and worldly lusts, we should live soberly, righteously, and godly, in this present world; looking for that blessed hope, and the glorious appearing of the great God and our Saviour Jesus Christ."* (Titus 2: 11-13)

The judgment seat of Christ is where it will be determined what we bring to the marriage supper of the Lamb. What materials we use are important. Gold, silver, and precious stones will survive judgment fire, but wood, hay, and stubble will be burned up.

Called to the Lamb's Supper

> *"And he saith unto me, write, blessed are they which are called unto the marriage supper of the Lamb."* (Revelation 19:9a)

We are to be joyful and thankful to the Lord, if we are truly saved and born-again, to be called to the Marriage Supper of the Lamb.

> *"And I John saw the holy city, new Jerusalem, coming down from God out of heaven, prepared as a bride adorned for her husband."* (Revelation 21:2)

The New Jerusalem or holy city comes down from heaven and will be in heaven. It

CHAPTER 2: WHAT IS MARRIAGE?

is a cube of four dimensions. God presents it down from heaven, ready and prepared just as a bride is prepared for her husband. The word prepared is in the Greek perfect tense. That means that this holy Jerusalem was prepared in the past, it is continuing to be prepared and goes on prepared into the future. The city is and will be prepared as a bride. It is not the Bride, but prepared as a bride. The Bride, the true saints, married to the Lamb will be forever with the Lamb in the heavenly city. This is a beautiful picture of the saving of a people for His name, a building of His Church, and a marriage between Christ, the Lamb of God and His Bride.

Song of Songs

If ever we could elevate and exalt our marriages the ideal to reach for is Solomon's Song of Solomon.

Chapter 1, Verse 1: *"The song of songs, which is Solomon's".* This song was written by Solomon and is one, likely the favorite, of one thousand and five that he wrote. *"and he spoke three thousand proverbs: and his songs were a thousand and five."* (1 Kings 4:32) This book is also known as Canticles. A Canticle is a little song. Most agree that there are five Canticles contained in Song of Solomon, but the new Scofield Reference Bible states there are thirteen.[1] The Song of Solomon is for the Christian who loves the Lord and loves the picture of the love between a married man and woman and the Lord Jesus Christ. This then should the Christian man and woman's personal book to help draw them closer to the Lord Jesus Christ.

Dr. McGee presents four important meanings found in his book, *Song of Solomon:*

1.) We find the glory of wedded love and the sacredness of the marital relationship. Real love between two people is shown, revealing the heart of a satisfied husband and a devoted wife. This is the opposite of what is found today where there is too much emphasis on sexual experience and there is not much known about love.
2.) The love of Jehovah God for Israel. The prophets spoke of Israel as being the wife of Jehovah. Idolatry was the breach that destroyed that unique wedding band.
3.) Gives a picture of Christ and the Church. The Church is the Bride of Christ, although not in view to Solomon, the Jews or the prophets, the

CHAPTER 2: WHAT IS MARRIAGE?

Song of Solomon is the picture of what is possible with human affection to convey this great love. Christ had to have had this inspiration to make all believers realize His wonderful love for us and to lead us into a newer and deeper relationship with Him as we have not known it before.

4.) Shows the communion of Christ and His saved ones. We are shown Christ's divine love for the individual and our soul's communion with our Creator. More than just experience, we are led into the personal relationship with Christ and are aware of His first love for us for which we love Him. Rekindling that real, live, burning passion for the person of Christ is His intent.

King Solomon

King Solomon reigned over Israel for 40 years and was known for his wisdom and prosperity. Solomon answered God when asked what He should give him:

> *"Give therefore they servant an understanding heart to judge thy people, that I may discern between good and bad:"* (1 Kings 3: 9)

> *"And there came of all people to hear the*

MARRIAGE, DIVORCE, & REMARRIAGE

> *wisdom of Solomon, from all kings of the earth, which had heard of his wisdom."* (1 Kings 4:34).

Solomon and his kingdom were greatly blessed with peace and prosperity for most of his kingly reign.

In the fourth year of his reign over Israel he began the building of the great Temple of Solomon, the house of the Lord. All was going well for King Solomon. King David, Solomon's father spoke these words about Solomon, his son of Bathsheba:

> *"Behold, a son shall be born to thee, who shall be a man of rest; and I will give him rest from all his enemies round about: for his name shall be Solomon, and I will give peace and quietness unto Israel in his days."* (1 Chronicles 22:9).

One thing that we can conclude, but have no scripture to back it up, is that King David must have taught Solomon something about the outdoors and nature. King David had a love for everything that God put here including him being a shepherd in his youth. He must have provided his son Solomon with studies in nature and on tending to the King's flocks. We can also conclude by further study that during this tender time of youth, Solomon met and fell in love with his first and only true love. We know that later on

CHAPTER 2: WHAT IS MARRIAGE?

Solomon accumulated seven hundred wives and three hundred concubines (1 Kings 11: 1 -3).

He wrote his own son about love in Proverbs 5:18:

> "Let thy fountain be blessed: and rejoice with the wife of thy youth."

Also he counseled:

> "Live joyfully with the wife whom thou lovest all the days of the life of thy vanity, which he hath given thee under the sun," (Ecclesiastes (9:9a).

King Solomon grew in wisdom, influence, and wealth.

> "So king Solomon exceeded all the kings of the earth for riches and for wisdom." (1 Kings 10:23)

But God warned Solomon not to swerve away from walking uprightly and to keep God's statutes and judgments. If Solomon would turn away from God and *"go and serve other gods, and worship them:"* (1 Kings 9:6B) He would judge Israel. But Solomon allowed his many pagan wives to lead him into serving and worshipping other gods and:

> "the Lord was angry with Solomon, because his heart was turned from the

Lord God of Israel, which appeared unto him twice," (1 Kings 11:9)

It must be noted that of all the myriad of wives and concubines attributed to Solomon only Rehoboam and two daughters are mentioned in scripture. In 2 Chronicles 12:13 it tells us that Rehoboam was 41 years old when he began his reign. He was born a year before Solomon's 40 year reign began. Rehoboam's mother was Naamah, an Ammonitess. Being in his late teens when he wed Naamah,[2] she must have been Solomon's first love, the wife of his youth.

The Song

Our love story begins with the bride's delight in and anticipation of the bridegroom's kisses. A kiss was a sign of peace and Solomon's name means peace. This is a very passionate and personal beginning to their relationship, the kind of peace extended from Christ to his followers through his salvation and words. The handsome couple followed by the virgin bridal attendants, depart and head for his chambers. The love they feel for each other far exceeds the highly valued wine that others cherish.

The bride has a moment of self-discovery. She is darkly complexioned, a

CHAPTER 2: WHAT IS MARRIAGE?

result of being burned by the sun while slaving in others' vineyards. But she is unkept and she realized it, just like her own vineyard. Her beauty is natural and comely. But in the presence of her beautiful husband she feels undone. This is the same as mankind who, quite frankly, is ugly. We are full of sin and all ugliness, what could possibly attract us to the Lord as we are. The Lord is going to make us an attractive bride and he has already started the work.

> "...Christ also loved the Church, and gave himself for it; that he might sanctify and cleanse it with the washing of the word," (Ephesians 5: 25, 26.)

The bride, who is a shepherdess, asks the shepherd about his flocks that she could not see. Sometimes we get apprehensive about what the Good Shepherd is doing. We want to know about other sheep when we should be only concerned about being His sheep. Also, back then it would matter to know whose flocks were whose so that any needless searching among strangers' flocks could be avoided.

In verses 8 thru 10 Solomon answers Naamah, Solomon's first love and wife. He calls her fairest among women, assuring her and all around that she belonged where she was, beside him and feeding her own flocks.

We are to be busy feeding on the words of God and Jesus expects the Bride of Christ to get out the Words of God to all around us. The bridegroom compares his love to a company of horses from Egypt. She has grace and strength. Her cheeks are lovely as jewels and her neck is as fine gold. In that time, and that culture you could not pay any higher compliment. He is totally infatuated with the inner and outer beauty of his bride. Christ will be very delighted with his adorned Bride in the same way.

While at the wedding supper table, (Verse 12), the bride's spikenard lets off a scent, which signifies the fragrance of Christ's life and what Naamah desires for their wedded life together.

Verse 13 says: *"A bundle of myrrh is my well-beloved unto me;"* The Myrrh speaks of Christ and the Bride's utter delight in His being. He should be with us in our hearts all through the day and the last thing to be with us at night. We can turn to Him with everything and be absolutely dependent and trusting in Jesus our Lord. He is our joy and ecstasy, and the Bride looks to her bridegroom with open eyes, opening that door to His grace and love.

My beloved is unto me as a cluster of camphire, says the bride. Behold, thou art

CHAPTER 2: WHAT IS MARRIAGE?

fair, my love; behold thou art fair, he says back to her. The love song is off to a splendid beginning, and we know in our hearts the love of Christ and His bride, the Church. The groom calls the bride pleasant (Verse 16). Having determined Naamah to be Solomon's first wife, her name means pleasant in the form of the Hebrew Language he used, being *naim*. It is an affectionate term used by him, a term from the heart expressing true comfort and satisfaction.

CHAPTER 2

Verse 1 is sung by the bride, Naamah. *"I am the rose of Sharon, and the Lily of the Valleys."* We usually think of these flowers as speaking of Christ the Lord. However, the bride is comparing herself to these humble and lowly flowers of the land, unworthy, as they were not to be in the royal gardens. However, Solomon turns that around and proclaims her as the Lily, beautiful, more beautiful than all the other attendants, the daughters of Jerusalem. She is more beautiful and his love and he wants her to know that and everyone present has to know that.

In verses 3 thru 7 the bride is musing about her love (Solomon) to the maids of Jerusalem. She compares Solomon to the fruit tree among wood trees. She gives him the praise and in such beautiful terms gives out what is in her heart about her beloved. It is a picture of Christ Jesus and his overshadowing of shade to protect us.

> "Keep me as the apple of the eye, hide me under the shadow of thy wings." (Psalm 17:8)

She thinks of being at the banquet and Solomon covers her with love. This is a beautiful picture of the marriage supper of the Lamb where the Church will be present. Naamah was in comfort and communion with Solomon, as we will be near Christ and in communion with Him. It will be a glorious time as the bride had with her bridegroom. She is feasting in love under his fruit tree tasting his sweetness. As we have tasted of the Lord:

> "If so be ye have tasted that the Lord is gracious." (1 Peter 2:3).

The precious gifts we have received of the Lord in the New Covenant have been purchased by His blood on the cross. We have been pardoned, His peace is in our souls, we are loved by Him, He gives us the joy of Holy Spirit and our hope is in eternal life. Solomon covered his bride with his banner of love. Christ has conquered us with His love, as was this young girl. From what

CHAPTER 2: WHAT IS MARRIAGE?

was before we were saved with until now His love has filled our souls and we remember our Lord's sacrifice with thanksgiving. In verse 5 the young woman professes she is overcome, sick of love, amazed and overpowered by it. Contemplating all that her lover has done for her, the kind person that he is, the love that makes her faint, it is all too much for her. David expressed this in Psalm 119:81:

> "my soul fainteth for thy salvation: but I hope in thy word".

The groom is there for his love embraces her in her love-sick condition. She rests in his strong hands gaining assurance of his love for her. The spouse gives a command to the daughters of Jerusalem, as if she is warning sin or even the devil, our adversary, to stay away. She is in love, love-sick, and in no way does she want that to be interrupted. Do not awake, this is better than a dream, she is locked in an embrace with him and him with her. Just as we are overcome with awe and love for our Lord, we want to be in the light of pure fellowship with Him, darkness stay away! There are times of intense, sweet, fellowship with Christ that we do not want to lose. There is only so much that our frail human hearts can take until we can be with Him uninterrupted forever.

In verses 8 thru 14 we have the heralded the return of Solomon, which the bride has been looking forward to. Recovered now from the near fainting Naamah hears the voice of her beloved. The Lord Jesus said:

> "*my sheep hear by voice, and I know them, and they follow me:*" (John 10:27).

We know Him through His words, and we trust Him. We will know Him when at the rapture we will hear Him.

> "*For the Lord himself shall descend from heaven with a shout, with the voice of the archangel, and with the trumpet of God:*" (1 Thessalonians 4:16).

That will be the voice of the beloved of the Church returning for His Bride. The Bride's beloved is on the mountain victorious, leaping and skipping to get to us. He is our way, as Solomon is for Naamah, drawing closer, getting nearer. We are waiting, she is waiting, and then he speaks. Rise up, my love, my fair one, and come away. The winter is past; long, cold, and forsaken. That's all gone, the rains of early Spring are gone. The earth is in bloom and warm again, her beloved is here. Whatever trials and troubles the young bride enduring

CHAPTER 2: WHAT IS MARRIAGE?

without her husband, they are a thing of the past. The Church's troubles can be sharp, but the Redeemer will return and all the troubles will be ended. After all that time when all seemed lost, attacks from the devil on all sides, when the time of frustration closed in, all of a sudden the time of the singing of the birds has come, even a turtledove's voice can be heard. The time of ripening arrives and Solomon calls to his bride, O my love. He is so glad to see her once again, to gaze upon her face and hear her sweet voice. It may be hard to imagine the Lord wants to see us and hear us, but He does.

Verses 15, 16, and 17 are a slight change to the young bride's idyllic thoughts. Little foxes, everyone was aware, could creep in and destroy the vines and their roots. These are subtle violations of God's Law, the devil's delight in tripping up believers over the smallest of things. There are little foxes everywhere trying to pull us away from our first love. The things that the Lord wants us to do, and we know to do them for Him but we don't.

> *"And he that doubteth is damned if he eat, because he eateth not of faith: for whatsoever is not of faith is sin."* (Romans 14:23).

Naamah all of a sudden became very concerned to not allow any little thing to interfere with the marital love between her and Solomon.

She redirects her attention to her beloved by confirming that they both belong to each other. There is close communion which is mutual between them. This relates to our interest in our Savior and Him in us, a mutual enjoyment with Him. We are in Him and He in us, it is the highest spiritual level that we can attain. It may be dark for us now because our Savior is not physically here but the night will be gone soon and the day will be here.

CHAPTER 3

Naamah is having a dream and she is in the City, presumably Jerusalem, and her loving husband is absent. Sleep is not necessary when she misses him whom she loves. This searching is indicative of when or if we lose fellowship or any connection with the Lord and the impulse is to find Him as soon as we can. Nothing else should matter. The help she received to find her mate was sure a relief. It should remind us of our search for the Lord to save us out of darkness, being led to Him by the Holy Spirit. Once she found her beloved she would not

CHAPTER 2: WHAT IS MARRIAGE?

let him go or get out of her sight. Jesus promised that he would be found by those that sought after Him with their whole heart.

Again for the second time the bride brings a charge to the daughters of Jerusalem, the virgin maidens. Don't allow your emotions to be stirred up to seek the wrong, ill-fated things of this wicked world's lusts. It must be the right time, the right place, and the right true love. Nothing that the bride is describing or anything else in this song is encouraging any sort of pre-marital sexual relations.

Versus 6 thru 11 give us a glorious glimpse of how it will be when the Lord returns for us. Solomon appears with his bride together entering into Jerusalem. The perfume of myrrh and frankincense, the aromas of Christ, envelop the bride. It is a majestic sight as the procession is escorted by sixty of the King's soldiers around the great wooden chariot, the seat within, carrying Solomon and Naamah was arrayed silver and gold with cloth of purple. Bathsheba, his mother, crowned him that day, as the still living, bed-ridden King David could not attend.

CHAPTER 4

This beautiful part of Solomon's song is

devoted to the deep, deep feelings he has for the bride. Everyone is to know how he feels about his beautiful bride. Does the Church even believe that Christ gives His highest commendation to her beauty? He begins by saying, thou art fair, my love. The bride had previous poured out her heart to him and now he takes the opportunity to return her favor, heralding to all to hear. Solomon uses rural country terms that both of them would be familiar with, being close to nature. Naamah's flowing hair to him is as a flock of goats from the mountain. She has nice even teeth that remind him of evenly shorn sheep. Everything about her is perfect in his eyes. Overall she is beautiful to him as Christ considers His Church as being beautiful. He knows us and we need not hide from Him but we can feel secure in bringing all our fears to Him. All of our beauty and value is derived from Christ Jesus. We have the incorruptible new, inner man, the holiness of Christ, and the hidden man of the heart are all inner beauties and are only the result of our Saviour's own beauty bestowed upon us. Our Lord puts a value on us as believers and expects gracious words of witness here on earth for Him. Solomon is enraptured by his bride's beauty, character, strength, and love.

Having respected his bride with praises for her outstanding features, Solomon

CHAPTER 2: WHAT IS MARRIAGE?

desires possession of his bride. Having fawned over her physical attributes: her eyes, hair, teeth, lips and mouth, cheeks, neck, and breasts it is time to sweep her away. They have already checked in with her mom and also Bathsheba, so now they are cleaving together. They have feasted together, as the Church will feast with Christ and we will know how much Christ loves us.

Solomon calls away his spouse and he calls her his spouse five times in verses 8-12. She willingly goes with him even through exhilarating dangerous areas. Up the hill of Amana which is the source of the Abana river, to Mount Hermon, snow-covered and a welcome relief from the sizzling hot city. Past the dens of leopards and lions, she is safe in her lover's arms. The Church is warned:

> "Be sober, be vigilant; because your adversary the devil, as a roaring lion, walketh about, seeking whom he may devour:" (1 Peter 5:8)

She has ravished his heart filling him full of joy, pleasures and happiness. They have shared intense, enrapturing delights. His soul is soaring. Everything is exciting him, fulfilling him, she is a whole garden of delights to Solomon. Pleasant fruits, spices, waters, and streams are all alive to him through the being of his spouse, his soul's mate.

Finally, in verse 16, the bride cries out to that north wind. It would be a pretty chilly one, being off the snowy peaks which are the bordering the anti-Lebanon range. This cold is needed to provide the flavors for the garden's peaceable fruits.

The Church needs the winds of adversity to flow, to produce in it the ripe fruits of righteousness. Naamah knows the south breezes and the warmth will come again and grow and mature the garden's fruits and spices. It will become a welcomed place for her beloved time and time again.

CHAPTER 5

Solomon has returned and is present in his garden in verse 1. He uses the term my sister, for Naamah, undoubtedly a strong, familial endearment as they have begun to become one flesh. It is a spiritual joining that they endeavor to explore, on top of the physical attraction that has remained so strong. Solomon had not gone far from his spouse and he was already busy in his garden. He has gathered spices, eaten honey from the honeycomb, and has drunk wine and milk. It's just like Christ being there at all times when we need Him, He is

CHAPTER 2: WHAT IS MARRIAGE?

never gone from our sides, we can always rely on Him. We desire our lord and it is the same, only more, that He desires us. This love, this marriage, this communion of souls can only be ordained by the Lord. The love Solomon and Naamah have for each other has as its source, the divine love of our God and Savior and His Living Waters.

> *"But whosoever drinketh of the water that I shall give him shall never thirst; but the water that I shall give him shall be in him a well of water springing up into everlasting life."* (John 4:14)

Solomon, speaking to his friends, with his bride asleep nearby is watching and waiting for her love with a heart awake. He comes to her *"open to me, my sister, my love, my dove, my undefiled."* Nothing in the heart is diminished, their love is at a high pitch for each other. He has been busy during the night, he is filled with the dew and his hair is wet with the night. The evening before has been filled with lovemaking and the merriment has made the madam sleepy, tired, and in an afterglow.

She has a complaint, a hesitation of being cleaned up, a usual custom of the time, before retiring. But (verse 4) she is moved with love for him as she rises to get the door. Our Lord Jesus Christ is always there knocking away at our hearts, arousing us to service when He deems necessary.

> *"Behold, I stand at the door, and knock:"*
> *(Revelation 3:20a)*

Naamah is overwhelmed for his love and rushes for the door. When she gets there he is gone. It was just in that hesitation that the moment was lost. Her heart must have dropped, *"my hands dropped with myrrh,"* but all is not lost. She found the fragrance on the door handle placed there by Solomon as an expression of his love and minor disappointment in not seeing her and not finding her awake.

Jesus comes to get us to do what He wants us to do. Sometimes believers are in a fog or wrapped up in self-filling activities, like sleep, to be useful. We lose our very close fellowship with Christ if we so much as take one step back from Him, or refuse to go where He wants us to go. If we get up and out we would find that sweetness of His perfume on our door handle resuming fellowship with Him.

Naamah is back in Jerusalem at this time and now she is frantic to join her beloved and shore up that fellowship. She leaves the palace, her comfort zone, to go look for him. We need to be in full fellowship with the Lord. If we have grieved the Holy Spirit with sin in our lives, or quenched the Spirit by not being obedient to God, fellowship is broken and our joy diminished. A big problem is being self-willed as a Christian and as a church so the sooner that it is realized that the will of God is not being done the better. If there is no joy in it there is no true fellowship as well. Naamah is out alone and pays the price for it. The watchmen who should be watching out for those within the city from those who want to hurt from without, do the hurting. She cannot find her beloved but is found by these men and is manhandled to her shock and dismay.

In verses 8 and 9, Naamah has eluded the rudeness of the night watchmen and finds friendlier confines with her friends, the daughters of Jerusalem. She wants them to tell her, to witness to her if they can, that when they find Solomon to tell him her heart is sick with love for him. She is frantic, missing her beloved husband, being attacked in the dead of night, and now having to beg these women whom she doesn't know all that well. Her heart is ready to place herself at the mercy of her husband, her every fiber of her being wants him above all, and that he must know that now, there is no time to be lost.

The response she gets is surely a heart-stopper. *"What is thy beloved more than another beloved?"* (verse 9). It may seem cold that they would sing to her that her special beloved is only special and beloved to her, so why should it be that way for them? An unkind blow, a severe knock, but it would be the same for an unbeliever or a religionist to inquire why Jesus means so much to you or me. Why does the Lord Jesus mean so much to the Church or to the individual believer? We must have the answer to that for unbelievers who are in darkness and very skeptical about any man, as they see it, that claims He is the Son or God and God the Son. God wants everyone to make a decision about His Son one way or the other. Everyone must decide. Everyone must decide if Confucius, Mohammed, Moses, Buddha, etc., are the Chosen ones, or that one of them is the Son of God, or if Jesus is just another prophet or who He said He was. Christians should know better that Christ Jesus loves us so much that He left all to die for all our sins and redeem lost souls. Christians must be ready to die for Christ and not let anyone or anything demean Him among all the gods of this world.

From verses 10 thru 16 we have the lovely bride's response in beautiful imagery about her beloved's kindness, his

CHAPTER 2: WHAT IS MARRIAGE?

thoughtfulness, his tenderness, and his strength. These women need to be told, they need to be enlisted for the search. Today if a child goes missing a whole army of people are enlisted of volunteers to search for the missing boy or girl. Cars, planes, 4-wheelers, dogs, and police fan out county-wide to leave no stone unturned. There are seven verses of detailed information about her husband she launches into. There has to be no mistake, the realness of her spouse's qualities must be made clear for these women. Her man is special and he needs to be found.

We must know our Lord ourselves if we are to defend Him. If we lose fellowship with Him we must repent and look for Him. He is not far. He wants us to cleave to Him, He wants that relationship with us. Naamah's responses about Solomon answer them.

In verse 10 he is white and ruddy and stands out among his peers. Our Lord is perfect and spectacularly white and red which denotes His righteousness and perfection and His perfect sacrifice in blood as the Lamb of God. Solomon was the greatest king on earth and our Lord Jesus Christ is the King of Kings forever.

Verse 11 speaks of a head of fine gold and perfect hair. This king of hers is kingly with the crown of gold and full of youthful vigor.

> "*I beheld till the thrones were cast down and the ancient of days did sit,*" (Daniel 7:9a).

The Lord is our treasure, our defense. His kingship shall be excellent above all others. The hair speaks of the beauty that was a young Solomon's.

She next describes his eyes as of doves by the waters of rivers. Our Lord's eyes burn with purity.

> "*Thou art of purer eyes than to behold evil, and canst not look on iniquity.*" (Habakkuk 1:13a).

A terror to enemies, harmless as dove's eyes is the Lord to those who love him. Solomon richly described Naamah as having dove's eyes, and now Naamah reciprocates.

Verse 13 describes his cheeks as spices and flowers, his lips like lilies, with the scent of sweet myrrh. Naamah likens Solomon and connects him with their gardens which are beautiful and sweet. The descriptions we have of our Saviour are pleasing to us and refreshing. There is nothing drab or ordinary about our Lord and we will be driven to great

CHAPTER 2: WHAT IS MARRIAGE?

heights of ecstasy when we finally lay eyes on Him. Solomon's kisses to his bride are pleasant and sweet and Naamah longs for them again. The combined images of lilies and myrrh show the complex impossibility of setting forth the utter beauty and excellency of Christ, we can only imagine and anticipate.

In verse 14 she raves about the hands and belly of her beloved. He is decked out with gold rings and precious stones in the finest settings. Diamonds must be present too but his hands alone appeal to the bride. Solomon works with his hands, commands with his hands and there is power in his hands. Naamah describes the true love from her husband as bright ivory with sapphires. Everything is described in lavish detail, as if the outward wealthy items are only a covering that cannot conceal what is underneath. It is the love itself that Naamah sees and feels. She is just forced to put it into palace terms for the daughters of Jerusalem to marvel at. There is unlimited value on the love between her and Solomon.

She continues in verse 15 to illustrate the strength of her man which only shows the radiance of her love for him. His legs are like marble, strong, his firm foundation. It is there, so exposed, so showy, so simple for her to express to him how much he elevates her. He is stable as set in sockets of gold. He is the foundation, the leader of the government, and it is anchored completely in him. He is assured and confident in her eyes.

We have a vivid description of the Saviour Christ Jesus given to us by John.

> "And in the midst of the seven candlesticks one like unto the Son of Man, clothed with a garment down to the foot, and girt about the paps with a golden girdle.
>
> His head and his hairs were white like wool, as white as snow; and his eyes were as a flame of fire;
>
> And his feet like unto fine brass, as if they burned in a furnace; and his voice as the sound of many waters.
>
> And he had in his right hand seven stars: and out of his mouth went a sharp two-edged sword: and his countenance was as the sun shineth in his strength."
> (Revelation 1: 13-16)
>
> "And he had in his hand a little book open: and he set his right foot upon the sea, and his left foot on the earth."
> (Revelation 10:2)

Our Lord will come again to the earth and take it over and put it under His power. He will come in all His magnificence.

CHAPTER 2: WHAT IS MARRIAGE?

Naamah describes Solomon's countenance as the whole beautiful country of Lebanon and his look as strong as the famous cedars from there. His was strong but our Lord is strong as the sun in all His brightness and fusion.

Verse 16 concludes this lavish praise with the mouth being as sweet as sweetness itself. For the bride it is delightful and graceful. She has put all her heart into forming this image of the beloved and all together he is to her very lovely. The same is the satisfying fullness of Christ Jesus for the believer. The more we gaze upon Him with our heart and eye of faith the more in awe we are in His complete person. He has given it all up for each one of us and He is precious to us. So there it is, Naamah's complete picture of her beloved to the daughters, and here is Christ in all his glory and magnificence to behold in splendor. The believer sings out, "I am yours, and He is mine." Naamah presents her beloved and her love and showed them how special and important he is to her. It is enough for them. It has to be.

CHAPTER 6

There is a change, the daughters of Jerusalem have gone from querulous apathy to ecstatic interest. They have snapped out of their early grumpiness and have come to the attention of the bride who is frantically seeking to recover heart sick fellowship with her spouse. In verse 1 the maidens realize that the king is being sought and they want to seek him also.

> "For he that cometh to God must believe that he is, and that he is a rewarder of them that diligently seek him." (Hebrews 11:6)

The maidens are all in to help the bride and are by her side. This buoys Naamah and in her mind and in her heart she reasons that her beloved has returned to his favorite place. He is at his duties and has not actually left his love to her own devices, but is assured in his heart she will appear. There is joy in her heart in verse 2 as she knows that shortly they will be reunited and her nightmare of broken fellowship will be over replaced by newly wedded love.

> "Ye have heard how I said unto you, I go away, and come again unto you. If ye loved me, ye would rejoice. (John 15:28a)

The Church rejoices and by faith seeks Christ Jesus by prayer and supplication at the throne of God. He is with the Father but is in us and the Church by His Spirit.

CHAPTER 2: WHAT IS MARRIAGE?

> *"This is the generation of them that seek him, that seek his face,"* (Psalm 24:6).

Verse 3 has the bride confirming the love they both have for each other to the maidens. It's a reconfirmation from 2:16, *"my beloved is mine, and I am his."* Her heart is settled and reassured. Our Lord reassures the Bride of the same love. He witnesses to the Father:

> *"And all mine are thine, and thine are mine; and I am glorified in them."* (John 17:10).

The Bride, which is the Church praises her Bridegroom:

> *"let us be glad and rejoice, and give honour to him:"* (Revelation 19:7a).

Our covenant and bond with God through the Lord Jesus Christ is renewed every day, every hour, and every minute, and we rejoice.

From verse 4 to verse 13 Solomon proclaims his bride as beautiful. He compares her beauty first to two cities dear to him and compares her to an army. You are beautiful "as Tirzah, comely as Jerusalem." Tirzah was a city inhabited by the tribe of Manasseh, and its name means pleasant. It was the capital of kings up to the time of Omri.

> "Began Baasha the son of Ahijah to reign over all Israel in Tirzah," (1 Kings 15:33).

It was a beautiful city and fit for kings. Comely as Jerusalem; the word comely, *neweh*, depicts something as beautiful, as a young woman is lovely. To Solomon, Naamah is a lovely woman and he is telling her so and that if she had any doubts or reservations about it to get over it.

> "Jerusalem is builded as a city that is compact together:" (Psalm 12:3).

It was a holy city and is the city of David and the city of God. The New Jerusalem, "which is above is free," (Galatians 4:26a) and is the home of the Church in the future. If comparison and praise to two cities is not enough, the bride is "terrible as an army with banners." (V4). In this verse and in Solomon's mind, terrible, *ayom*, means in a loving way awesome and majestic. Her beauty was such that it could over power a man, as when someone in that time would witness a large army marching with all its flags and banners.

Then the King repeats his love imagery from chapter 4, verses 1-3, about her hair, teeth, and temples. See my love, nothing has changed, he's reassuring her, all is as

CHAPTER 2: WHAT IS MARRIAGE?

before. When the Christian stumbles out of fellowship, Christ picks him/her up and says your beauty is stunning. We are stunned that He feels the same and if we repent He is very pleased. Again, the simile of her hair is reminding Solomon of a group of goats descending the mountain, and her teeth as a flock of freshly shorn and washed sheep are well-known terminology and endearment to Naamah. Her cheeks and forehead are beautifully colored as a slice of pomegranate. This imagery of animals and fruit may seem over the top, and it may not have been this mushy for these two in reality, but it points us to the perfect love the Saviour has for His bride, the Church. He died for the Church and is cleansing and sanctifying it:

> *"that he might present it to himself a glorious church, not having spot or wrinkle, or any such thing; but that it should be holy and without blemish."* (Ephesians 5:27).

Verse 9 picks up with his bride being the only daughter of her mother, whom he met before and was approved. Now Solomon puts her on a pedestal, above all other women as far as he can see. He presents Naamah to them and they all return the praise to her. He sums her up as fresh as the morning, a light in the night, bright as the sun, and repeats her overwhelming effect as an army marching, arrayed for battle. (verse 10).

In verse 13 Solomon invites his bride to return to him after this short hiatus. Return, return is the constant refrain from our Lord Jesus. He is always there if we ever turn our gaze away from Him. He redirects us back to Himself, no questions asked, just the continuous washing of the word for His Bride, and a constant check by our Saviour on the work begun in our hearts and souls. It is a Church that is built up and joined together with Christ as His Bride that all will see.

CHAPTER 7

As an inference from the previous chapter to the word company in verse 13 meaning a dance or dancing, Naamah in the beginning of this part of the song is performing for her spouse. From the Hebrew *holah*, the word denotes "a joyous time with rhythmic moving of her body just for her husband." ...the women came out of all cities of Israel, singing and dancing," (Samuel 18:6). *"Is this not David, of whom they sang one to another in dances"* (*holah*) (1 Samuel 29:5).

The first nine verses tell of Solomon being spellbound and enraptured by the

CHAPTER 2: WHAT IS MARRIAGE?

beauty of Naamah. The assurances are past, the bride wants her all to be given to her spouse. In fact, in this dance of love by Naamah she is totally unclad, *in puris naturalibus*. The effect on Solomon is startling and immediate. He shows his appreciation for her dance by the description of her beauty as they are very alone together for this private affair.

Solomon in verse 1 comments on her feet being beautiful to him with or without shoes. He starts with her feet and is going to work up to her fair head. The Lord has dealt with the human race saying that he would curse Israel, *"from the sole of thy foot unto the top of thy head,"* (Deuteronomy 28:35b). It's the same complete coverage here only it's in wonderment of the bride by the groom. The Lord considers us the same way as we are in our bodies now. He heaps honor upon us, *"and those members of the body, which we think to be less honourable,... God hath tempered the body together, having given more abundant honour to that part which lacked."* (1 Corinthians 12:23, 24). We feel honored in that from our Lord, but Solomon heaps honor and love upon the very members of his bride who dances on. He says her thighs are perfect like jewels made by a cunning workman.

The next metaphors concern her round navel and her belly or overall body as the best milled wheat with lily flowers. It was in good health that he sees it in his eyes as:

> "It shall be health to thy navel, and marrow to thy bones." (Proverbs 3:8).

Her body is going through many motions, it is affecting Solomon, overwhelming him and adding to the moment.

Verse 3 has the first mention of her breasts which shows that she is unclad and revealing to him. He compares them to two young deer or does that are twins, even and equal to each other.

In verse 4 Naamah's neck previously was likened to a tower of David, rigid and strong. Here is a comparison to a tower of ivory, white and precious and very politically incorrect. The saints by the neck are jointed to Christ the head of them. Her eyes are like the fish pools at Hesbon. In the simile before her eyes were the eyes of doves. Heshbon was a Moabite city east of the Jordan River. The Gate of Bath-Rabbim opened toward Rabbah in Ammon. The ponds or fish pools by the gate which held fish, glimmering with reflections would intentionally please Naamah, her being from that nearby area.

CHAPTER 2: WHAT IS MARRIAGE?

Her nose being compared to a tower of Lebanon denotes pure and perfect structure. Lebanon then was known for its beauty, and the name Lebanon has as its meaning, white, using Lebanon as a symbol shows the beauty, strength, and pride that existed in his bride. Most towers back then were used as military watchtowers and fortified posts. Solomon, though at peace, would use military terms, especially in this case. Facing Damascus we can see the steadfastness and determination of the militant Church in fending off false prophets and teachers in the name of Christ.

Verse 5 starts with Solomon admiring her head like carmel, a name for which has as one of its meanings, garden. For its understanding, adjectives such as fruitful and plentiful are used. This prominent headland, was bounded on the south by the Bay of Aire and was near the Mediterranean. It was a lovely garden spot where Elijah slew the prophets of Baal. It would be no accident that in these exquisite pictures of Naamah that the idea of gardens would be present. Much of their lives involved and revolved around gardens as places of beauty, retreat and pleasure. Naamah's hair receives special attention as it is likened to purple. The queenly threads of royal purple form her crown and top her off beautifully.

The King is in his galleries may be explained in Psalm 132, verses 13 and 14.

> *"For the Lord hath chosen Zion; he hath desired it for his habitation. This is my rest forever, here will I dwell; for I have desired it."*

Solomon, being King could have been anywhere in the kingdom and with anyone else and doing anything else. He is expressing his total satisfaction with Naamah, his true love. As the Church is lovely in the eyes of Christ, so is the bride lovely and acceptable to the king.

He roars his excitement for his bride, *"How fair and how pleasant art thou, O love, for delights."* (V6). In this dance, in this time for all the senses to be aroused, he cannot but be enraptured in ecstasy and pleasure. Christ has put His comeliness upon the Church and is very pleased in her. In summing up the experience, Solomon is in a heightened state of emotion and Naamah has spent this whole time in dance affirming her same exact feelings for him. Even in the next verse (7) he's summing up her total beauty as a figure like a palm tree, straight in lines with beautiful fronds of green. Another reference to her breasts as clusters of grapes or possibly dates from the palm is exciting him.

CHAPTER 2: WHAT IS MARRIAGE?

In verse 8 Solomon lets it all out and exclaims that he will go up to the palm tree, her straight, perfect figure. It is a picture of taking his wife, taking hold of the boughs thereof. He has delicately described a time of no more constraint, the time of intimate lovemaking has come for him and his bride. They both bask in the love for each other as if they are the best of wine for each other. Their love is enough for themselves, and if only others could experience it for themselves it would cause those who are asleep to awake and speak about love.

Solomon has given Naamah expressions of his ardent love as Naamah has willfully submitted to her husband with joy. Their fulfillment in each other has fueled and inflamed their total desire for each other. The Queen gives her faithful utterance to her beloved, *"I am my beloved's, and his desire is toward me,"* (verse 10). His desire is passionately and entirely for her. The Church submits to Christ in full faith and trust and victory. The Church joyfully directs her love and admiration to her Saviour, *"I am my beloved's."* The confidence she shows in Christ leads to *"I am thine, save me;"* (Psalm 119:94. The true desire of the Church will be forever with Christ the Lord. God said, *"and thy desire shall be to thy husband, and he shall rule over thee."* (Genesis 3:16b).

The Church willingly submits to the Lord.

The last three verses lay out a path that the bride desires they travel in their continued wedded life at least for the near future. They both want the feelings to last and grow. Having sexual relations for their own sake is not practical. The physical and spiritual joining is what's desirable. Solomon and Naamah had three children, with Rehoboam becoming king of a diminished kingdom. God has shown us the practicality and the beauty of marriage in the Song of Solomon. He has shown us how we can understand His love for His Church. We give God glory for saying:

> "marriage is honourable in all, and the bed undefiled: but whore-mongers and adulterers God will judge." (Hebrews 13:4).

Marriage was meant by God to be delightful and fulfilling for the couple. If two people, Solomon and Naamah for example, honor God in marriage, God is pleased and blesses that union. However, any deviation outside the bounds and into any of the forms of fornication displeases Him and He will judge but will also forgive upon repentance.

CHAPTER 8

This last section of the song takes place in the countryside. A visit to the bride's family is what she wants to cement her communion together with her spouse. She hopes for a sweet, good time with her husband. Her home was in the country of the Ammonites and they run up against her older brothers and Naamah laments that if Solomon was a brother she would not be despised by them. Being with the King of Israel did not benefit the bride everywhere, all the time. The Church is espoused to the Lord Jesus Christ and desires a free and close relationship to be appreciated by all. It just does not work out that way. The Church is despised for her love of the Saviour and persecuted for it. Nevertheless, that does not stand in the way of the Church's desire to be in closer communion with Jesus Christ and be identified with and made one with.

> *"For both he that sanctifieth and they who are sanctified are all of one: for which cause he is not ashamed to call them brethren,"* (Hebrews 2:11)

"When I should find thee without," is what Naamah means, if in open company when not alone with her husband, she would kiss him in an open display of love. If he was her brother she would not have that limitation, but she is being bullied and intimidated by her brothers. Now the Church has Christ and is not ashamed to show love and affection towards him, nor should there be any fear of open display.

"*I would lead thee,*" in verse 2. Naamah says as she freely wishes to show everything in her mother's house to him and to hold nothing back. Nurturing the relationship with her husband is first in her heart. The Lord instructs His people for He desires them not to be ignorant. The Lord implants His soul and His Spirit upon His people who are open to Him, to share in His knowledge of His words.

> "*My people are destroyed for lack of knowledge.*" (Hosea 4:6).

She would have Solomon drink the spiced Pomegranate juice form her own pomegranates. The Lord will drink the new wine with the Church in the new covenant.

> "*But I say unto you, I will not drink henceforth of this fruit of the vine, until that day I drink it new with you in my Father's kingdom.* (Matthew 26:29).

In verse 3 Naamah pines for her lover's hands around her and to be embraced by him. But with the forced graciousness of familial familiarity, the strain it was causing

CHAPTER 2: WHAT IS MARRIAGE?

did not allow any fanciful dalliance. The support of Christ for His body of believers can be depended on and trusted but never taken advantage of.

> *"And when I saw him, I fell at his feet as dead. And he laid his right hand upon me, saying unto me, fear not; I am the first and the last:"* (Revelation 1:17).

Verse 4 contains the third charge from Naamah to the virgin maidens about pre-marital sex. In Song 2:7 Naamah tells them to save themselves for their husbands in the future. She did and reaped the benefits of staying pure in her virginity. This was quite an achievement in her country which was immensely immoral. Surely, in the case of the Jewish maidens of Jerusalem they would face death if it was discovered that they were not virgins on their wedding night.

Verse 5 has an unknown relative with the first sighting of the married couple who are quickly identified. Her leaning on him conveys the love this wedded couple has for each other to the family. Her mother is quick to take the credit for "awakening thee" to the upbringing she would need when she would meet and marry a husband. The Church was raised up from lowliness and persecutions by the grace of God the Son. "Rejoice, thou barren that bearest not;...for the desolate hath many more children than she which hath a husband. (Galatians 4:27).

Verses 6 and 7 are a back and forth exchange between Solomon and Naamah. Remembering her mother's upbringing she urges him to seal his promise to her of complete love and fidelity. She wants to be that very seal to his heart and upon his arm of strength. She wants a permanent place in her husband's heart. This is also symbolic of the Church's desire above all to be bound only to the love of Christ. Christ assures us,

> "In whom ye also trusted, after that ye heard the word of truth, the gospel of your salvation: in whom also after that ye believed, ye were sealed with that Holy Spirit of promise." (Ephesians 1:13).

Naamah reaffirms that her love is strong as death for Solomon. This love invokes a violent, zealous, passionate fire.

> "...but that he loved us, and sent his Son to be the propitiation for our sins." (1 John 4:10).

"Jealousy" is a fact and an emotion that can eat us up or help us grow. Those that love God must be zealous against idols or anything that would draw us away from His love. Naamah was zealous of her love for Solomon and realized that there would be

CHAPTER 2: WHAT IS MARRIAGE?

many women attracted to him. Her devout affection and ardent love for her husband is such a "vehement flame" which burns so bright in the bride. The fire must not be threatened nor be diminished for the love of Christ that the Church has for Him. It is a powerful fire in each of the members of the body's souls. It is a holy love and holy fire in the sanctified hearts of the Bride for Christ.

Solomon answers Naamah in verse 7. It is a passionate, reaffirming love in his heart that just swallows up and embraces his wife. No amount of water, rivers, or tributaries would be able to quench his love for Naamah. *"Quench not the Spirit"* (1 Thessalonians 5:19) we are told, let the fire of the Holy Spirit burn in our hearts. No waters or floods or tribulations can quench our love for our Lord. It is strong and it is powerful. Solomon's love is also like a fire for his wife and he promises that their love is worth more than all his kingdom. At the time Solomon was the richest man ever up unto that time, and in today's value would still be the richest man to have ever lived. He had money, fame, the most wisdom, and to him the most love in the world.

The last two verses are like the solemn vows that Solomon and Naamah made in their marriage. It is the culmination of all their physical attraction, love of God and spiritual communion of their two souls merging as one flesh. This would be the ideal model of marriage in the heart.

The visit to family nearly over, the family converges to update the news. They are very protective and relate how they are caring for and preparing her for that right time when she will be betrothed. They will build for her if she is behaving in a proper way, like Namaah did as she saved herself for Solomon. If she acts like a loose woman they will rein her in.

In verse 10, Naamah repeats before her family that she was a virtuous woman before she met her husband. She was chaste and favored before him when that proper time came. The Church values itself when it finds favor in the Lord. This causes happiness and joy in its growth and guidance by the Lord through the Holy Spirit. To the Church at Philadelphia Christ said "Because thou hast kept the word of my patience, I also will keep thee from the hour of temptation" (Revelation 3:10a).

Solomon in verse 11 is shown by his bride to have a vineyard at Boalhamon, of which the location is unknown. The word means Lord of the multitude, and this vineyard was one of possibly a thousand that

CHAPTER 2: WHAT IS MARRIAGE?

he had. It was let out to keepers and parallels the parable of the vineyard in Matthew 21:33-41. Each of the vineyards was to bring a price or earning for the rent. Each believer is given a vineyard and is charged with bringing forth fruit out of that vineyard. We are to do our service to God in our vineyard but we are to remember that it all belongs to God.

In the last two verses Naamah and Solomon turn to each other and she desires to hear his voice by his directing himself to her. The visit and business are done. He can now return and lavish all his attention on her. They met and began in the gardens and they shared happy times together in the gardens, and it is fitting that Solomon's Song leaves off in the gardens.

Throughout this beautiful song the interactions of love between Solomon and Naamah lead one to see the similarities between Christ and His love for the Church which are the born-again true believers. It is a physical, emotional, and spiritual depiction of marriage as Christ intended it. At its very end the Bride is saying to the Bridegroom to return. The Bride at the very end of the book of Revelation says, *"Even so, come, Lord Jesus"* (Revelation 22:20b)

The true love that Jesus intended for

marriage comes through in this song and in His Scriptures. It is that the husband and the wife were to be one in flesh and in spirit, to have joyful physical love along with spiritual love and everything else in between. It was to be one man and one woman for life, as long as each was alive. There was to be no alteration to that law. From the beginning this was to be so. As presented here in this song, the physical delights of two (a man and a woman) joined together in marriage are to be enjoyed regardless if the union produces children or not. Our prayer should be to fulfill to the best of our abilities, with God's grace, His purpose for us.

CHAPTER 3

THE JUDGMENT SEAT

A discussion about the Bema Seat or Judgment Seat of Christ is very relevant. In light of Peter Ruckman's views on the doctrine of marriage, divorce, separation, and remarriage it is very important. In Ruckman's book on marriage he states: "it is Bible doctrine. If you don't accept it, you're the sinner. (emphasis his). Your problem will be how to justify yourself at the Judgment Seat of Christ."

Funny, he of all people, should bring up the Judgment Seat of Christ as if it were a light thing. Funny he should be so off the cuff about something so serious as our Saviour's dealing with believers' works for Him. Especially for Mr. Ruckman, a man divorced twice, married three times, and still in the pulpit.(Update: Ruckman is now retired from the pulpit.)

Matters of Mercy

"For we must all appear before the judgment seat of Christ; that every one may receive the things done in his body, according to that he hath done, whether it be good or bad." (2 Corinthians 5:10)

> "...that ye may have somewhat to answer them which glory in appearance, and not in heart." (2 Corinthians 5:12b)

Every action as God's child during a lifetime must be judged by the law of righteousness which is embodied by Jesus Christ. Every believer will be rewarded according to good and bad works in their lives. We are encouraged in the word to judge our own selves here and now. Jesus said: *"and yet if I judge my judgment is true:"* (John 8:16a)

Since we are knowledgeable of the coming judgment of the saints we should as honest Christians call ourselves to account for those things we have been doing wrong. In a spirit of repentance we can continue to please God in accordance to our human purpose.

> "But when we are judged, we are chastened of the Lord, that we should not be condemned with the world." (1 Corinthians 11:32)

A lot of the bad can be alleviated now before the Bema Seat takes place.

> "For if we would judge ourselves, we should not be judged." (1 Corinthians 11:31)

It makes a lot more sense to humble

ourselves before Christ and be strengthened in body and soul, instead of being weak and sickly by resisting what Christ provides in truth to us. We should thank God that He provides us such an opportunity to make our reward full. To refuse the chastisement of God undermines His grace.

We endure the present chastening of the Lord in order to partake in His Holiness.

> *"Now no chastening for the present seemeth to be joyous, but grievous: nevertheless afterward it yieldeth the peaceable fruit of righteousness unto them which are exercised thereby."* (Hebrews 12:11)

The Seat

The inevitable reality of the appearance of Christians before Christ at His judgment seat becomes clear as we understand from Scripture its purpose. The judgment seat was prevalent especially in Roman times.

Solomon made a judgment porch of cedar from which he could impart his wisdom in judgment.

> *"Then he made a porch for the throne where he might judge, even the porch of judgment; and it was covered with cedar from one side of the floor to the other."* (1

Kings 7:7)

It evolved to the formal chairs or benches where judges or governors would hold court and give judgments. We see the judgment seat in its Roman use as Pilate judged Jesus to death. The Jews threatened Pilate if he let Jesus go he would be exposed as a traitor.

> *"When Pilate therefore heard that saying, he brought Jesus forth, and sat down in the judgment seat in a place that is called the Pavement, but in the Hebrew, Gabbatha."* (John 19:13)

> *"Then delivered he him therefore unto them to be crucified."* (John 19:16a)

Another example of the use of judgment seats in Roman times involved the apostle Paul. Gallio was the deputy of Achaia when the Jews rioted against Paul. The Jews brought Paul to the judgment seat, but Gallio drove them away.

> *"Then all the Greeks took Sosthenes, the chief rules of the synagogue, and beat him before the judgment seat. And Gallio cared for none of those things."* (Acts 18:17)

The Greek word, *bema*, is used ten times in the New Testament for judgment seat. The judgment seat of Felix, the

CHAPTER 3: THE JUDGMENT SEAT

procurator of Judea, where Paul was tried, was in the government house in Caesarea.

Standing Before Christ

> *"For the Father judgeth no man, but hath committed all judgment unto the Son:"* (John 5:22)

Jesus Christ will be the One judging Christians at the judgment seat. This He does gladly for He loves His own and wants to reward them. All Christians will be examined by Christ for their service to Jesus Christ after salvation. The believer stands saved and will not be judged for salvation.

> *"Wherefore we labour, that, whether present or absent, we may be accepted of him.*" (2 Corinthians 5:9)

It is what we do after being saved and up to the time we appear before Him that is to be judged. It is the work completed in us that was begun in us at salvation and upon completion of that work.

> *"Now he that planteth and he that watereth are one: and every man shall receive his own reward according to his own labour."* (1 Corinthians 3:8)

All the things we have done since salvation will be made manifest, or brought out into the light. At that precise moment those things will be tried by fire to see which works were for Christ.

> *"Every man's work shall be made manifest: for the day shall declare it, because it shall be revealed by fire;"* (1 Corinthians 3:13)

> *"Is not my word like a fire? saith the Lord; and like a hammer that breaketh the rock in pieces?"* (Jeremiah 23:29)

Good or Bad Works?

The foundation for our works is the foundation of the Lord Jesus Christ. We need to be careful as to how we build upon this foundation. There are certain materials we should be using and those that we shouldn't be using.

> *"Now if any man build upon this foundation gold, silver, precious stones, wood, hay, stubble;"* (1 Corinthians 3:12)

These are figurative terms that represent important things. Using such things as wood, hay, and stubble will be tried by fire of the word and reduced to ashes. It will become apparent that those things of man and impressive to man are worthless to the Lord and will account for nothing. Such as mega churches that glorify man and compromise God's words with modern Bibles will be destroyed. This is sad since many

CHAPTER 3: THE JUDGMENT SEAT

Christians believe in the modern social gospel, contemporary Christian music, and the lowering of all Godly standards. These works will be burned and those will experience loss, but will be saved.

We all need to be exhorted to do those things that will abide, being built upon that solid foundation. Gold, silver, and precious stones are representative of those works which will stand for Christ. These will be counted for reward and value for eternity. We can glorify God by manifesting these works for Christ.

Gold, Silver, and Precious Stones

Ignoring the corruptible wood, hay, and stubble works, let us strive for the gold, silver, and precious stones that God will accept.

> *"Now if any man build upon this foundation gold, silver, previous stones, ..."* (1 Corinthians 3:12)

What are some of these things that will have value eternally and are considered in God's eyes to be gold, silver, and precious stones? From David Cloud's *Encyclopedia of the Bible*, we can list some:

1. Faithful church membership. (1 Timothy 3:15; Hebrews 18:25)

2. Being a loving, providing husband. (Ephesians 5:25)
3. Being a submissive, serving wife. (Ephesians 5:22)
4. Being an obedient child. (Ephesians 6:1)
5. Gospel preaching, winning souls to Christ and world evangelization (Mark 16:15).
6. Raising Godly children according to Proverbs 22:6.
7. Walking in the Spirit and not the Flesh. (Galatians 5:25)
8. Being filled with the Spirit (Ephesians 5:18).
9. Seeking God (Hebrew 11:6; Proverbs 8:34, 35).
Sacrificing for Christ (Mark 10:29).
10. Approving excellent things. (Philippians 1:10).
11. Being pure in spirit and body (2 Corinthians 7:1).[1]

This is my no means all, and we could include: walking in fellowship with Christ day by day, maintaining a fruitful prayer life, delighting in and reading God's words, loving Christ's Church, being zealous in Christ's work, separating form the world's evil, and false doctrines and false teachers, and giving according to your needs.

CHAPTER 3: THE JUDGMENT SEAT

Crowns

A crown is a chaplet wreathed about a brow to highlight that brow from others, a symbol of rank, and seal of inherited or achieved distinction, valued quite apart from its own intrinsic worth.[2]

The value of a crown is for what it implies rather than for what it is. The word used for crown means an achieved crown awarded for personal victory. This victory is in Christ, the believer powered by Christ to win the race set before us by Christ. It is His achievement, He has done all the achieving through weak vessels like us.

The actual Greek work for crown is, *stephanos*, from *stepho*, to twine or weave; a Chaplet, a prize in public games or a symbol of honor. There are many races in the world that give a prize. For the Christian it is the high calling of Jesus Christ that we strive for.

> *"Now they do it to obtain a corruptible Crown; but me an incorruptible.:* (1 Corinthians 9:25b)

The Five Crowns

After our works as Christians are judged according to Christ as being worthwhile or whether they are worthless, rewards in the form of Crowns will be given.

> *"And when the Chief Shepherd shall appear, ye shall receive a crown of glory that fadeth not away."* (1 Peter 5:4)

The rewarding of crowns takes place after the rapture at the Judgment Seat of Christ. There are five crowns listed in the Scriptures.

The Crown of righteousness.

This will be awarded for those who love His appearing when finally it will be total joy to be in His presence. (2 Timothy 4:8)

If a believer has lived righteously in the Lord and are dedicated to being watchmen for the coming of the Lord he/she will receive this Crown.

The Crown of Glory.

This Crown is for pastors who have faithfully preached the Word and properly fed the sheep. Those who have served for filthy lucre or Lord it over the brethren with heavy burdens or yokes upon the necks of the saints will not receive this crown. God put a great importance and value on those who preach and teach other Christians. (1 Peter 5:4)

CHAPTER 3: THE JUDGMENT SEAT

The Incorruptible Crown

> *"And every man that striveth for the mastery is temperate in all things. Now they do it to obtain a corruptible crown; but we an incorruptible."* (1 Corinthians 9:25)

This is the crown all believers are running for in the race, in order that they may obtain. Jesus died and imputed His righteousness to believers. He overcame carnal desires and all selfish desires and gives us the power to live right for Him. We use the power of Christ to compete for righteousness in our life to show how thankful we are to Christ Jesus in saving us. Therefore, there is no shame.

The Crown of Life

This is the suffering crown. We are to suffer as saints in Christ. We are killed all the day long as long as we live on earth.

> *"Blessed is the man that endureth temptation: for when he is tried, he shall receive the Crown of Life, which the Lord hath promised to them that love him."* (James 1:12)

This is referred to as the Martyr's Crown. Saints are to remain faithful to Christ unto death. If we fail in that we will lose this crown. Endure hardness, trials, tribulations, even severe suffering, sometimes unto death. This is the greatest courage and love that we can show God.

The Crown of Rejoicing

> *"For what is our hope, or joy, or crown of rejoicing? Are not even ye in the presence of our Lord Jesus Christ at his coming?"* (1 Thessalonians 2:19)

This crown has been called the soul winners crown, for those who are faithful to the witness and the leading of souls to Christ. Paul is our greatest example of soul winning, and if we can do a fraction of the work Paul did for Christ we will be rewarded. Christ gives us the tools and the power to turn every opportunity the Lord gives us to turn lost souls to Him.

These are the rewards our Lord has ready for us. We play by the rules to win to bring the fullest glory possible to our Lord Jesus Christ. Any self-righteousness or thought of personal gains will disqualify us. Our motives and heart need to be pure in the Lord.

CHAPTER 4

PORNEIA

This chapter fills a need for an understanding of two particular terms the Lord Jesus uses in regards to the subject of divorce. It's the sad truth that as the Lord did explain that man-made divorce was a direct result of man's hardness of their hearts that this terrible subject needs discussion. The crucial text of Matthew 19:9 contains the two terms that will be discussed; fornication and adultery.

> *"And I say unto you, whosoever shall put away his wife, except it be for fornication, and shall marry another committeth adultery: and who so marrieth her which is put away doth commit adultery."*
> (Matthew 19:9)

It should be brought out that the term put away had the same meaning as divorce. Two forms of the word divorce are used in the New Testament; divorced the perfect participle and divorcement (as in writing of) the noun. They are used a total of four times. The term put away is used sixty-two times in the New Testament and comes from the Greek, *apoluo*. The first time we find its use is in Matthew 1:19:

MARRIAGE, DIVORCE, & REMARRIAGE

> "then Joseph her husband, being a just man, and not willing to make her a publick example, was minded to put her away privily."

In those times the person that was put away, or divorced, was considered the innocent one. The Jews thought that the one who was unjustly divorced was falsely stigmatized and guilty of immoral behavior. Deuteronomy 24:1 states:

> "when a man hath taken a wife, and married her, and it come to pass that she find no favour in his eyes, because he hath found some unclean-ness in her: then let him write her a bill of divorcement, and give it in her hand, and send her out of his house."

This bill of divorcement was dismissed and cleared by the mate establishing the wife as the innocent mate by being given a bill of divorcement. If the wife was guilty of fornication then according to the law she was stoned and not granted a bill of divorcement.

> "Then they shall bring out the damsel to the door of her father's house, and the men of her city shall stone her with stones that she die..." (Deuteronomy 22:21a).

Now Joseph wanted to put away Mary but she was not guilty of any wrongdoing.

Joseph's suspicions were answered by an angel's message in a dream to him.

The Greek, *apolelumenen*, is used in Matthew 5:32 for an innocent, unjustifiably put away wife who was not given a written bill of divorcement which is the same as a Certificate of Innocence. She has to carry the stigma of being guilty and as if she was an adulteress. Thus if a man would marry this innocent but stigmatized women, he has adultery committed against himself.

We see the same thing in Matthew 19:9. This wife was also put away, just dismissed by the husband for any reason. She must, without a writing of divorcement freeing her, walk around as if she is an adulteress. This man in this verse (v9) marries another woman. The Greek verb, *moichatai*, means that he commits adultery against himself since his innocent wife is dismissed and he was remarried to another woman. The woman he gets married to becomes an adulteress due to his actions.

Fornication

Very simply, fornication is the voluntary sexual intercourse between a man and a woman not married to each other.

Dr. Henry M. Morris defines it as: "the

Greek word for fornication *porneia* could include any sexual sin committed after Biblical usage, 'fornication' can mean any sexual congress outside monogamous marriage. It includes premarital sex, adultery, homosexual acts, incest, remarriage after un-Biblical divorce, and sexual acts with animals, all of which are explicitly forbidden in the law as given through Moses (Leviticus 20: 10–21). Christ expanded the prohibition against adultery to include even sexual lusting (Matthew 5:28)[1]

A few definitions of the Greek noun, *porneia*, and the verb, *porneuo*, are as follows:

    4202 Porneia (por-ni'-ah) from 4203; Tant

    1) illicit sexual intercourse
    1a) Adultery, fornication, homosexuality, lesbianism, intercourse with animals, etc.
    1b) Sexual intercourse with close relatives. Leviticus 18.
    1c) Sexual intercourse with a divorced man or woman; Mark 10:11,12
    2) Metaphorically; the worship of idols.
    2a) of the defilement of idolatry, as incurred by eating the sacrifices offered to idols.
    4203 Porneuo (porn-yoo'-o)

CHAPTER 4: PORNEIA

1) To prostitute one's body to the lust of another.
2) To give one's self to unlawful sexual intercourse.
2a) To commit fornication.
3) Metaph. To be given to idolatry, to worship idols.
3a) to permit one's self to be drawn away by another into idolatry.²

So then fornication is illicit sexual intercourse outside of marriage, often said particularly by an unmarried woman. The flood was sent by God as judgment against the human race on account of the wickedness (spiritual and physical) of man. (Genesis 6:5-7)

Tamar, the daughter-in-law of Judah, childless, disguised herself as a prostitute and by soliciting Judah committed fornication which bore twins.

Tamar, daughter of King David and brother of Absalom, was raped and committed fornication with Amron, another son of David.

The shameful wife of Potiphar, with her infamous advances to Joseph to seduce him would have led him to commit fornication. But Joseph resisted, *"how can I do this great wickedness, and sin against God"* (Genesis 39:9b). Joseph defines fornication as a great

MARRIAGE, DIVORCE, & REMARRIAGE

wickedness and a sin against God. The principle or moral purity with its source being God is always sufficient for any situation that immorality rears its head.

Fornication, as well as adultery, bestiality, and sodomy were severely condemned in Mosaic Law (Leviticus 20: 6-21) and most offenses of this kind were punished by death.

In the New Testament, Paul attests to the social corruption existent in his time in Romans 1:26-32. "Fornication" is often used figuratively for spiritual idolatry. "For from within, out of the heart of men, proceed evil thoughts, adulteries, fornications, murders" (Mark 7:21).

> *"Plead with your mother, for she is not my wife, neither am I her husband: let her therefore put away her whoredoms out of her sight, and her adulteries from between her breasts."* (Hosea 2:2).

Adultery

Adultery is sexual intercourse with someone other than one's husband or wife. Adultery the noun is from the Greek, *moichao*, from *moichos*, an adulterer.

The main uses for the word adultery are found in Matthew 5:32;19:9 and Mark

CHAPTER 4: PORNEIA

10:11,12.

> Matthew 5:32 says
>
> *"But I say unto you, that whosoever shall put away his wife, saving for the cause of fornication, causeth her to commit adultery: and whosoever shall marry her that is divorced committeth adultery."*

The wife in the passage has been put away or dismissed from the marriage for whatever reason. She is the innocent party of that union and has not been given a writing of divorcement.

> *"Whosoever shall put away his wife, let him give her a writing of divorcement.:* (Matthew 5:31).

Since she does not have such a writing of divorcement, as was the custom to do in those days, she would walk around condemned as an adulteress. If the man in Matthew 5:32 as in 19:9 has had sexual relations with other women and dismisses his wife, then she herself has not committed adultery. The husband who has dismissed his wife for any reason then commits adultery against her. This is undeserved adultery on her part, but the Scripture says that anyone marrying the put away wife assumes her adulterous state and is an adulterer. This type of stand says that the innocent woman who was dismissed by her cheating husband and not issued a bill of divorcement clears her of extramarital sexual sin. She continues, however, to bear the societal stigma and assumed guilt of being an adulteress because of her husband's actions and inaction.

Those in Matthew 5:32 and Matthew 19:9, says another side, are Jewish families under Jewish law. There it is said that the couple were espoused and not yet married. It was during this espousal period that the writing of divorcement be issued and the marriage (they were considered married) dissolved. These were cases of fornication before marriage, or pre-marital sex, but espoused. There is no Jewish type espousal period for us today, and these verses make it clear that there are no exceptions.

Today's Reality

> "For the woman which hath an husband is bound by the law to her husband so long as he liveth; but if the husband be dead, she is loosed from the law of her husband. (Romans 7:2)

> "So then if, while her husband liveth, she be married to another man, she shall be called an adulteress: but if her husband be dead, she is free from that law; so that she is no adulteress, though she be

CHAPTER 4: PORNEIA

married to another man." (Romans 7:3)

"And he saith unto them, whosoever shall put away his wife, and marry another, committeth adultery against her. And if a woman shall put away her husband, and be married to another, she committeth adultery." (Mark 10:11, 12)

"whosoever putteth away his wife, and marrieth another, committeth adultery: and whosoever marrieth her that is put away from her husband, commiteth adultery." (Luke 16:18)

There needs to be a comment on all this. In order to justify some beliefs about marriage and divorce a reshuffling of terms seems necessary. For example, John Owen states that adultery is fornication. Christiananswers.net also says that adultery is fornication. These two terms adultery, *moichao*, and fornication, *porneia*, are two completely different terms with different meanings and are, therefore, mutually exclusive.

Does Porneia Mean Fornication?

An interesting side light is the summary of Bruce Malina in his paper, "Does Porneia mean fornication?":

"To sum up: Porneia means unlawful sexual conduct, or unlawful conduct in general. What makes a particular line of conduct unlawful is that it is prohibited by the Torah, written and/or oral. Pre-betrothal, pre-marital, non-commercial sexual intercourse between man and woman is nowhere considered a moral crime in the Torah. Aside from the instance of R. Eliezer, there is no evidence in traditional or contemporary usage of the word Porneia that takes it to mean pre-betrothal, pre-marital, heterosexual intercourse of a non-cultic or non-commercial nature, i.e., what we call fornication today." [3]

Malina footnotes that summary by saying:

"A further question, beyond the scope of this short article would be: to what extent was non-commercial, pre-betrothal, pre-marital heterosexual intercourse possible in the various cultural groupings in the 1st century? Would the general marriage age of girls preclude such a possibility?"[4]

It does say in Leviticus 19:29:

"do not prostitute thy daughter, to cause her to be a whore, lest the land fall to whoredom, and the land become full of wickedness."

All the way back in Genesis 38:24 there were great penalties for fornication:

"Tamar thy daughter-in-law hath played the harlot; and also, she is with child by whoredom. And Juda said, bring her forth, and let her be burnt."

CHAPTER 4: PORNEIA

> *"And whosoever lieth carnally with a woman, that is a bondmaid, betrothed to an husband, and not at all redeemed, nor freedom given her; she shall be scourged;"* (Leviticus 19:20)

> *"And the man that lieth with his father's wife hath uncovered his father's nakedness: both of them shall surely be put to death; their blood shall be upon them."* (Leviticus 20:11)

> *"And if a man lie with his daughter-in-law, both of them shall surely be put to death."* (Leviticus 20:12a)

> *"And the daughter of any priest, if she profane herself by playing the whore, she profaneth her father: she shall be burnt with fire."* (Leviticus 21:9)

The penalties in the law for *porneia* (fornication) were grave and severe and carried out. They were not just dismissed as casual trespasses. They were grave sins and mostly punished by death so as the land would not be defiled before God.

Hillel and Shammai

Hillel and Shammai were two leading Jewish Rabbis of the early first century who were founders of opposing thought, known as the House of Hillel and the House of Shammai. Between the two, three to five disputes are mentioned in the Talmud.[5]

The House of Shammai was known as having the stricter interpretation of the law and the House of Hillel the more moderate. It was the character of its founder, Hillel, quiet, peace-loving, accommodating and determined to bring man nearer to their God, that reflected a more liberal tone. The ones in the House of Shammai tended to be stern and unbending like their founder, Shammai. The Shammaites could not be stringent enough in their trying to enforce the law upon everyone. The followers of Hillel were peaceful and gentle and as such were able to weather the upheavals suffered in Israel. The House of Shammai took no back seat in going after any and all that went along with or promoted any type of friendly relations with the Romans. Whenever measures of political or social conflictions ended up in the Sanhedrin governing body, it was usually the Shammaites plus the Zealots that won out.

The Men

Hillel became one of the most influential people in Jewish life. He studied and worked as a woodcutter. Known for his poverty, kindness, gentleness, and concern for humanity he established his organization of academies of learning all known as the

CHAPTER 4: PORNEIA

House of Hillel. Hillel was the more popular of the two Rabbis and that was because of his soft, compliant, accommodating spirit.

Shammai the elder was a native of Israel as Hillel was born in Babylon and migrated to Israel. There is not too much known about Shammai the man except that he was in construction and was known for his authoritarian views. He was known for having a temper, gloomy, and inpatient.

Both lived during Kind Herod's reign (37-4 BC) when Roman rule prevailed in Israel. The source of Shammai's strict interpretation resides in his mind that the more the Jews interacted with Romans the more the Jewish culture, etc., would be compromised. Hillel did not share this fear so he was much more liberal in his interpretations. After Menahem the Essene had resigned the office of Vice-President of the Sanhedrin, Shammai was elected to the post, Hillel being at the time president.[6]

On Divorce

The House of Shammai said that a man may only divorce his wife for a serious transgression, but the House of Hillel allowed divorce for the most trivial of offenses, such as burning a meal.[7]

The theory of the law that the husband could divorce his wife at will was challenged by the school of Shammai.[8]

This authority in the Jewish family to divorce a wife at will originated when Hagar was dismissed by Abraham.

> *"And Abraham rose up early in the morning, and took bread, and a bottle of water, and gave it unto Hagar, putting it on her shoulder, and the child, and sent her away: and she departed.* (Genesis 21:14)

This right of the Jewish husband to divorce his wife at will formed the central column for the entire Jewish divorce system. It took until the 1200's to abolish this absolute right. The time during which the husband could divorce his wife at will was known as the Mischnaic period. It was the Shammai school of thought that challenged this, saying that the husband could not divorce his wife except for the cause of sexual immorality. Naturally, the School of Hillel countered by saying any act on the wife's part that displeased the husband would be grounds for the issuance of a bill of divorcement. The School of Hillel's liberal stance prevailed with Philo of Alexandria and Josephus agreeing. The problem escalated as more and more Jewish husbands just dismissed their wives without a writing of divorcement.

Bill of Divorcement

The Hebrew bill of divorcement is known as a "get". The wife's right to sue for divorce was unknown to Biblical law.[9]

She still does not have the right to divorce her husband but a court must decide if she is entitled to be divorced from her husband and force him to give her a "get".[10]

When a "get" was first used is not known, except it goes back to the times of Abraham and was well known by the time Deuteronomy was written. (Deuteronomy 24: 1-4). In early times the procedure for a "get" was simple, only requiring dates, place, and the names of the two parties. It would usually just state simply "thou art free to any man" (Git 85b)[11]

> *"It hath been said, whosoever shall put away his wife, let him give her a writing of divorcement."* (Matthew 5:31)

Even today the "get" is a result of an order from the husband. One person that he directs writes it, while others he may bring in witness to the bill. There is a form used today which was described by Maimonides. There are no conditions written into the "get", but the husband only may impose conditions on the wife at the delivery of the "get". Traditionally, ten men including the rabbi, the witnesses, and the scribe act together to deliver the "get" to the woman. The woman is divorced as soon as she takes delivery of the "get".

BETROTHAL

The position of betrothal as it pertained to Jewish relationships and to how scripture is interpreted today is held by many good pastors here in the United States and elsewhere. According to Dr. D.A. Waite,

> "Matthew 19:9 describes a Jewish practice of betrothal. During that state, the man was called a husband, and the woman was called a wife. There was no sexual intercourse between them. This betrothal was very binding. It could only be broken by a divorce and the only grounds for such a divorce would be if the other partner had committed fornication. If there was a putting away or divorce during this betrothal period, (unless one party had committed fornication) followed by a marriage, this would involve adultery. This is why fornication and adultery are used in the same verse. They are separate concepts with separate meanings. They are not the same as many Bible teachers and pastors teach."[12]

To add a clarification, Dr. Waite says:

> "The so-called exception clauses of

CHAPTER 4: PORNEIA

> Matthew should never contradict the clear teachings of Mark, Luke, Romans 7, and 1 Corinthians 7. These verses in Matthew 5 and 19 deal with the practice of the New Testament Jews regarding espousal. When a Jewish man and a Jewish woman were espoused (betrothed) (as Mary and Joseph were), that espousal could only be broken by divorce if either party had committed fornication with another person. There was no legal marriage up to this point. The divorce simply broke up the espousal relationship between these two people. The words adultery and fornication must be used in their distinctive meanings and cannot be taken to be synonyms. The first deals with sexual infidelity on the part of someone who is married. The second deals with sexual infidelity on the part of someone who is merely espoused."[13]

In general, the betrothal, also called espousal, is a formed state of engagement to be married.[14]

In Jewish weddings from the first century before Christ to the sixth century after Christ there were two ceremonies. The first was the betrothal "erusin" with the wedding the second, usually a year apart. From the 13th century on the two ceremonies took on the format of a combined public ceremony. The betrothal is today a part of the Jewish wedding. This happens with the groom giving the bride a ring. Betrothal is separate from engagement in Judaism and breaking of a betrothal requires a divorce and the violation of betrothal is considered adultery.[15]

To further clarify for today. According to Torah law, a marriage is a two-step process. The first stage is called Kiddushin, loosely translated a betrothal, and the second step is known as Nisu'in, the finalization of the nuptials[16].

In an article from 2008 David W. Jones tackles the Betrothal question, entitled, "The Betrothal View of Divorce and Remarriage." He briefly states as an introduction the lack of a consensus of Church leaders on what is taught in the Scriptures about divorce and remarriage. There are several surveys on the matter and they all hinge on their interpretation of the exception clauses in Mathew 5:32 and 19:9 and particularly the definition of "Porneia". In many texts on marriage and divorce, the betrothal view is either dismissed or just mentioned in passing.[17]

Jones then defines the view: This interpretation holds that with the exception clause Jesus was referring to the unique Jewish practice that allowed for a marriage to be annulled if evidence of infidelity was manifest during the betrothal period.[18]

CHAPTER 4: PORNEIA

No matter who reviews or writes about betrothal, pro or con, everyone agrees the position to be a credible interpretation. It has never been the majority view in the Church but it has been present for centuries, literally since Abrahamic times.

The proper or improper interpretation of the word *porneia* is then the main separation point between the three main views of the exception clauses. There is an unlawful marriage view, a majority view, and the Betrothal view. So, if there is an exception for divorce it would bolster the two other views and not the Betrothal view.

CHAPTER 5
PHYSICIANS OF NO VALUE

"But ye are forgers of lies, ye are all physicians of no value." (Job 13:4)

In this chapter two southern personalities are covered in regard to the majority view of the exception clauses is concerned. Perhaps the clauses do not make much difference to these two individuals, but something should due to the chaos and havoc wrought upon the Church in the name of Jesus Christ by them. This is not meant to be an ad hominem attack on anybody but a reproof of some very despicable actions which should never be in the name of our holy Lord and Saviour.

Job pointed the finger at his so-called friends, calling them liars and, *"miserable comforters"* (Job 16:2). Believers are hurting and suffering in many ways. Then Satan comes and fills the believer with fear and fear-mongering leaders have their guards down and there is no stand taken against all the wiles of the devil. Satan's ministers of deception are infiltrating and destroying everything good in sight and Churches fall by the wayside. The physicians are giving lessons and answers contrary to the word of God. They are bound to be of no value to the Children of God presenting the wisdom of man full of lies and deceit. Their solutions are based on politics, economics, education, philosophy, sociology, religion, and especially psychology.

Mixing truth and error these natural brute beasts entrap saints when at the same time violate God's divine principles. They speak evil of the truth which they understand not. They have brought damnable heresies into the Church and deny the Lord, the Lord that bought them. In this day then, we are besieged as were the people of Israel in Jeremiah's time.

> "Is there no balm in Gilead; is there no physician there?" (Jeremiah 8:22a)

Saints are in dire straits, looking to their leaders of the Church for a cure and find only physicians of no value. The situation is desperate and is only a precursor to what is to come. The Truth of Jesus Christ, the gospel message, the message that everyone is a lost sinner is a fading, faint whisper today.

> "And they will deceive everyone his neighbour, and will not speak the truth: they have taught their tongue to speak lies, and weary themselves to commit iniquity." (Jeremiah 9:5)

CHAPTER 5: PHYSICIANS OF NO VALUE

Today many wolves in sheep's clothing fit this description and prescription of physicians of no value. Beware of megachurch personalities such as Joel Osteen who command thousands upon thousands of hungry souls. Preaching a feel-good, works and faith mixture for a gospel, deceiving so many unaware of the methodologies being employed to short-circuit God's unalterable principle found in Holy Scripture.

Are the Pentecostals or Charismatics the ones to run to and seek out for help and Bible feeding in these last days? All the false healings, false tongues and false miracles will only disillusion sincere seekers with a heart looking for God. Their renewal spirit of experience disregards truth and they only aid the fast approach of the one-world church, in the ecumenical movement together with Rome. This movement is filled with physicians of no value.

The New Evangelical Movement which split from Fundamentalists in the 40s was born out of a spirit of compromise and a rejection of Biblical separation. This includes the advancement of inclusiveness and friendliness with the ecumenical movement in Rome. "Evangelicals and Catholics together" was an ecumenical compromise signed in 1994. Started in the 70s during the Ford administration, collusion between Falwell's Moral Majority, Francis Schaeffer and son with Rome thru the Carter years culminated in the total capitulation in the nineties until now. Today we have day-to-day ecumenism. Embracing humanism, psychology, and pragmatic approaches to ministry, this movement promotes unsound fellowships and is riddled through and through with good-for-nothing physicians of no value.

Many, many fundamentalists qualify today as being physicians of no value. Militancy is gone in exposing the false teachings of Roman Catholicism, and any and all apostate churches. They compromise with disobedient brethren and bring in contemporary Christian music, modern Bible versions, and lower standards.

God tells us that we are not to work with or associate with evil doers but separate from them.

> "Ye that love the LORD, hate evil:"
> (Psalm 97:10a).

That is a command from the Lord which most preachers are not following today. If we fail to hate the evil we will fall prey to the evil and evil doers.

CHAPTER 5: PHYSICIANS OF NO VALUE

"Let him eschew evil, and do good; let him seek peace, and ensue it." (1 Peter 3:11)

Southern Shame

Who would have thought that people in the Bible Belt, the South, the home of Family Values, would register the highest rates of divorce in the country?[1]

As the new south expanded from the 1970s, nearly 65% of marriages have been destroyed. Divorce grew in the rest of the U.S. during the 1990's but restrictions still held true in the South. The evolving attitudes of religious people in the South followed the ups and downs of the Rev. Charles Stanley marriage. In May of 2000 the Stanley's divorce was announced. Even though Rev. Stanley told the Church he would leave the pastorate if he became divorced, it was applauded by the congregation when it was announced that he would continue in that position.

Old Mores vs New Mores

It wasn't always this way in the South. Divorces were few and far between. What was most common would be for feuding couples to split up and go their own separate ways. New relationships would ensue, with or without the benefit of marriage.

The ones who were married in the old South would see the man as head of the family and the women and children no better off than his property. The woman had no asset rights and could not refuse her services to her husband. Out of this arrangement came the tradition of the Southern Belle, the woman that needed protection, restriction and costly care with no legal standing.

After the Civil War southern attitudes about divorce changed drastically. Slaves were freed and the concept of women and children as being property changed too. Divorce was not widespread during this time in the south. People were frightened with the fear of God in this regard. If couples could no longer progress in their marriage they just split up and began new relationships without the benefit of marriage.

World War II brought more changes to marriage and relationships in the South. Women experienced more freedom from their husbands as a result of men serving overseas. They worked in the factories and tilled farmland. Women who cared for themselves and their children were reluctant to see an end to that freedom at war's end. Divorces skyrocketed between the 1960s and 1980s and they were made even easier by

CHAPTER 5: PHYSICIANS OF NO VALUE

no-fault statutes adopted by many southern states.

It had gotten so bad since the 60s that sociologists and others have renamed the "Bible Belt," the "divorce belt." The Sunbelt states of the South, which have been changing rapidly for decades have also registered the highest divorce rates. From the Carolina's to Oklahoma and from Florida to Kentucky resides twenty-nine percent of the nation's population accounting for thirty-five percent of all divorces.

Even though divorce rates have fallen recently, this is only a result of fewer marriages. Many are opting for living together and splitting up if it doesn't work out. Assets are needed to be divided up also.

Barna Research reported in a survey that born-again Christians in conservative congregations had a higher divorce rate than non-Christians. Appallingly, there are studies saying that Baptists are among the most divorced Americans.

> "Conservative Christians are more likely to get divorced than any other faith group. Baptists get divorced at a higher rate even than atheists."[2]

Under discussion now will be two so-called born-again Christian leaders who have been married and divorced multiple times. One is residing in a deep southern state and the other in a not so deep southern state. The geographical and socio-economic circumstances will not be discussed here, but the effects of such actions on the Church are supreme and cannot be dismissed.

The first is Mrs. Gail Riplinger.

Gail Riplinger

Gail Ludwig Latessa Kaleda Riplinger is a known author and speaker. But she wasn't always known by her five names. For years and years people only knew her as Gail Riplinger. Hers is a sad but classic story about how a Christian is not supposed to act when it comes to marriage. Hers is a story of lies, deception, tale-bearing, scripture twisting, marriage, divorce, and remarriage.

Everything is documented in Pastor D.A. Waite's book entitled, *A Warning! On Gail Riplinger's KJB and Multiple Inspiration Heresy* and Kirk Divietro's, Th.M., Ph.D., book *Cleaning Up Hazardous Waste.*

First of all Gail Riplinger, Peter Ruckman, and others that follow them hold to a heretical view of the inspiration of the Scriptures. They hold to the view that the King James Bible, a Bible translation, was

CHAPTER 5: PHYSICIANS OF NO VALUE

inspired by God through a second time inspiration process. God breathed out of his mouth and in 1611 those English words became the King James Bible. Since they believe in this heresy of the verbal plenary inspiration of the King James Bible they supplant and degrade the inspired Hebrew, Aramaic, and Greek words given by God himself. Mrs. Riplinger also teaches that since Act 2 there have been multiple inspired versions of the Bible in addition to the inspiration of the King James Bible. She states in her brochure, *Hazardous Materials,* that the Greek texts, including the Textus Receptus do not reach the level of perfection as does the King James Bible.

We find in Luke 17:3, "take heed on yourselves: If thy brother trespass against thee, rebuke him; and if he repent, forgive him"

> *"These things speak, and exhort, and rebuke with all authority, let no man despise thee."* (Titus 2:15)

These commands will be clear when we further investigate Mrs. Riplinger.

It is very obvious to see that Mrs. Riplinger is very angry and bitter as you read her words in *Traitors,* and in her book *Hazardous Materials.* The revelation that she has been married three times and divorced twice has triggered a rage to well up inside of her.

Up to that time Mrs. Riplinger had taught in many churches on the Bible version issue. There were men present in the audience. She has justified this anti-Biblical action by identifying herself with Old Testament women who were righteous and used of God. She has felt that she is on a mission from God to slay the Bible issue defenders and do so in the name of God from the pulpit in front of men. Pastors had previously had her speak when she knew that God does not allow women to teach and speak in the pulpit. She taught in churches and subjected her own husband to her authority, and no preacher corrected her. Men must always in the Church show up to take responsibility for leadership which God has given them. God has given the guidelines for the Church in the Scriptures.

1 Timothy 2:12 says:

> *"But I suffer not a woman to teach, nor to usurp authority over the man, but to be in silence."*

There should be the proper authority in the Church as given by Christ. He is the head and the covering over the man and the man

CHAPTER 5: PHYSICIANS OF NO VALUE

the covering of the woman. To be in Christ the proper order in the Church as instructed by Christ must be exercised. Paul instructed Timothy about the proper conduct and the proper order in Christ's Church. When the man is in authority in Christ within the home over the woman, Christ does not turn around and allow women to usurp authority in the Church over men.

> *"For God is not the author of confusion, but of peace, as in all churches of the saints."* (1 Corinthians 14:33)

The question is why did pastors, who had to ask questions about the Bible from a woman, not follow Biblical Commands about women and Church order?

> *"Let your women keep silence in the churches: for it is not permitted unto them to speak; but they are commanded to be under obedience, as also saith the law."* (1 Corinthians 14:34)

The answer lies in the fact that Mrs. Riplinger kept the information about previous marriages and divorces close to the vest. She neither informed the congregations she taught in front of, nor did the pastors who invited her know anything was amiss (or did they?). It was all a web of deceit and lies, which no born-again Christian should ever find themselves in.

Besides, much of what she teaches is dead wrong. She is wrong about the preservation of God's words. She believes that we have no preserved words that God gave us. Everything was just updated by God into contemporary vernacular until God breathed out His words in English which is the King James Bible. Her thesis is summed up as follows:

"As a result of this process every Holy Bible", Mrs. Riplinger's term for the authoritative Bible in a given language, "is free standing". The meaning of its words does not extend back past the production of that Bible. The reader should determine the meaning of the words of Scripture by using methods described in "In awe of thy Word," her book) for example, simply by reading ten words before and ten words after. These Holy Bibles are made up of Holy Ghost given "holy separate from sinners' vocabulary." It would be sacrilege to try to define or expand on them to make them more understandable to the modern reader."[3]

Besides her heresies on the Bible and teaching of men, the main point of contention of this present work entails her anti-Biblical marriage, divorces, and remarriages.

CHAPTER 5: PHYSICIANS OF NO VALUE

Lies and Deceit

Mrs. Riplinger has attacked Pastor D.A. Waite, Th.D., Ph.D. who is a world renowned teacher, Scholar of Hebrew and Greek, and Pastor in Collingswood, New Jersey. He has tirelessly defended the traditional Hebrew and Greek texts of the Bible, as well as the King James Bible. He is the husband of one wife, father of five children, and numerous grandchildren and great grandchildren. No one can point to any failure in any area of his Christian walk. Yet he has come under direct, bitter and disrespectful attacks by Mrs. Gail Riplinger. She has cast dispersions on him and his ministry as a pastor.[4]

She has disparaged his scholarship and Jacobean academic qualifications unmercifully.[5]

She has led a harsh verbal attack on Dr. Waite's leadership in the area of doctrine and Bibliology by calling him a "cardinal."[6]

She has given false accounts of his publications, his family, his friends, with the subtle intimation of lying in them.[7]

She has shown disrespect and dishonor for the Waites who are her seniors by many years. She has lied to her friends, Dr. and Mrs. Waite, about her marriages, and she has called them liars many times.[8]

Every charge brought by Mrs. Riplinger has proven false or has been refuted. Spurgeon has said:

> "no one ought to be made an offender for a word; but, when suspicion rules, even silence becomes a crime."[9]

Be prepared for a vigorous response by Dr. Waite to the false and sordid charges made by Mrs. Gail Riplinger.

Who is Gail Riplinger?

Gail Riplinger was born Gail Anne Ludwig in late 1947.[10]

She was 26 in 1973. She filed for her first divorce plus a legal separation on October 17, 1974.[11]

The first divorce became final on February 10, 1975.[12]

When she was 36 years old she filed for her second divorce,[13] which became final on August 6, 1984.[14]

She has many people believing that her divorces took place before she was saved. If we can take her word for it, she was 26 years old when she got saved.

CHAPTER 5: PHYSICIANS OF NO VALUE

"I received the Lord Jesus Christ as my Savior when I was 26 years old..."[15]

"I was saved as a graduate student (at Kent State University)....and 26 years old by the time I'd gotten saved."[16]

Her first divorce and legal separation was filed on October 17, 1974, days after her 27th birthday. She was saved when she was 26 years old in 1973. Her divorces were first of all of an unscriptural nature. In early 2008 she had told Dr. and Mrs. D.A. Waite that she had never been married to any other man than her current husband, Michael Riplinger. She was not in any process of divorce after her salvation, she was still a Roman Catholic by her own admission. She had lied and covered up her two divorces when asked by the Waites. She has lied to the Church at large and deceived everyone by posing as someone that was only married once to one man.

She is a public figure giving many lectures and teachings, influencing hundreds about her books and materials. Would all those deceived Christians have chosen to be influenced by her if they had been told the truth? Keeping her divorces secret belies her belief of harboring no guilt about lying about them. Lying about sin is an abomination to God. Those who are leaders in the Church must take measures before God so as not to be out of line and become disqualified.

> *"Holding faith, and a good conscience; which some having put away concerning faith have made shipwreck:"* (1 Timothy 1:19)

> *"But I keep under my body, and bring it into subjection: lest that by any means, when I have preached to others, I myself should be a castaway."* (1 Corinthians 9:27)

Mrs. Riplinger lied to churches all through the 1990's, especially when she lectured a group of pastors at Gospel Light Baptist Church in Walkertown, North Carolina. She told them that while a professor at Kent State she was not married.

To the congregation of Temple Baptist Church in Knoxville, Tennessee, she said the same thing. She repeated at a pastors' conference in 1994 that she had no one to support her.

The truth is that for the first half of her professorship at Kent State she was legally married to her second husband, Franklin Kaleda. For approximately the last half of her professorship at Kent State she was married to her present husband, Michael Riplinger.

What sort of issues would Mrs.

CHAPTER 5: PHYSICIANS OF NO VALUE

Riplinger face if people knew of her divorces? The first thing that it would do would be to close Church doors to her. No lectures, no teaching in churches, no fees. Therefore, if there were closed doors to Pastor's churches there would be less and less of her books that would be purchased, a great source of income to her. People have a right to know the truth about someone, especially if they are investing in their books and materials. She knew then that she was lying about her divorces and continued on as if she had done nothing wrong.

> *"Such is the way of an adulterous woman; she eateth, and wipeth her mouth, and saith, I have done no wickedness."* (Proverbs 30:20)

When Mrs. Riplinger lies about her unscriptural divorces, she left her first two husbands, she has lied to every Christian who tries faithfully to follow God's law of marriage and to whoever has purchased any of her books.

Waite Interview, 1995

Mrs. Yvonne Waite, wife of Dr. D.A. Waite, conducted a widely viewed interview with Mrs. Gail Riplinger in 1995. In this interview Mrs. Riplinger stated that she knew her current husband, Michael Riplinger, for a

MARRIAGE, DIVORCE, & REMARRIAGE

year prior to their marriage.[17]

Therefore, she met Michael Riplinger nearly eight months before filing for divorce from Frank Kaleda, becoming final on August 1, 1984. On September 4, 1984, less than one month after her second divorce became final, Gail Ludwig and Michael Riplinger applied for a marriage license. Whatever went on between the two in the eight months before Mrs. Riplinger was divorced the second time satiated their desire to marry two months removed from the second divorce.

Mrs. Waite asked Gail Riplinger how she met her current husband, Michael.

> "Ah, one of my students became a Christian; I led her to the Lord. And she had a brother that had never been married. And she started praying that her brother would meet someone like me. That's all she said, that he'd meet someone like me – I don't know why, you know, she thought I was all right, or whatever, but. And, so, he, he-she moved away, and his mother invited me over to dinner at that house and I went over. And, ah, I met him.[18]

Here we have a married woman going to dinner with intentions to meet another man. Mrs. Waite then asked Mrs. Riplinger if she fell in love with Michael Riplinger and married him right away? Her answer:

CHAPTER 5: PHYSICIANS OF NO VALUE

> "Well, I think it was within a year, or something like that, that, ah, we were married... but the Lord is – He has His timing, and it just breaks my heart when I see people not waiting for the Lord's timing on things, you know?[19]

We'll never know if she fell in love with Michael, not having answered the question put to her by Mrs. Waite. Her meeting Michael, in October 1983, would have been well before her divorce from Mr. Kaleda in August of 1984, just two months before their marriage. Mrs. Riplinger completely forgot to tell Mrs. Waite in the interview that she was married and divorced from her second husband before being married to Michael Riplinger. In her answer to Mrs. Waite about meeting Michael Riplinger at dinner she left out that she was still married to Frank Kaleda. She did mention emphatically that Michael had never been married before. This perhaps was a hidden message that people may register in their minds that since he was never married maybe she too had never been married. That would not be such a great leap to make. Perhaps Mr. Kaleda should have been invited to the same dinner. Is there a pattern of deception here? She was meeting another man at the man's mother's house at least six months before she filed for her second divorce. She gave Mrs. Waite and all that were listening in 1995 the impression that Michael Riplinger was indeed her first husband. And she also gave the Lord the praise for bringing her current husband into her life for which she had abandoned her spouse. It can safely be said that the Lord had nothing to do with such a nefarious scheme. That scheme was, of course, to meet and marry Michael Riplinger and abandon and commit adultery against Mr. Frank Kaleda. It was not the God of the Bible to whom she refers.

> "Ye are of your father the devil, and the lusts of your father ye will do. He was a murderer from the beginning, and abode not in the truth, because there is no truth in him. When he speaketh a lie, he speaketh of his own: For he is a liar, and the father of it." (John 8:44)

This seems very clear coming from the mouth of our Lord Jesus. His words have not passed away, and he meant them to mean exactly what he said then, through our time, and into the future. That's what the future perfect in Greek means. Perhaps this is the reason that Mrs. Riplinger has no love for the Greek as we have it written in the Textus Receptus.

> "So then if, while her husband liveth, she be married to another man, she shall be called an adulteress:" (Romans 7:30)

CHAPTER 5: PHYSICIANS OF NO VALUE

Gail Riplinger will live as an adulteress as long as her husband is alive. God's words have not and will not change for any of us, no matter how much we want them to. This is the state of her living in the eyes of God, this is her disqualification for most of the ministries she has been involved in.

As Mrs. Waite continued on in her interview with Mrs. Riplinger, she had no clue at the time who the real Gail Riplinger was. She was in no trite heart to confess this fault to Mrs. Waite or to any of the pastors she had duped. Listen to how Mrs. Waite described the secretly conniving Gail Riplinger:

> "You're very beautiful.... I don't know what I had expected, although Dr. James Sightler had said you were a picture of what a Christian woman should look like and act like, which was very nice... I think when men meet you, they probably are taken back a little because they probably expect sort of a feminist-looking person, and you're feminine and you appear to be very dear."[20]

It seems clear that Mrs. Riplinger has a hard time with telling the truth and a problem with God's truth. She appears to be a kind, nice, sweet, soft-spoken, Christian person. She appears to be what she needs to be to appear as someone that pastors may want to speak in their Churches. She gains peoples' confidence and trust by telling them

MARRIAGE, DIVORCE, & REMARRIAGE

pretty much what they want to hear, smooth things, which she is good at. For Dr. Sightler to fawn all over her is a disgrace and not a sign of discernment on his part. She shows such a false face and uses so much deceit, it is hard to imagine how Christians led by the Holy Ghost would be so duped.

> *"Lying lips are abomination to the Lord:"* (Proverbs 12:22a)

We have been warned as Christians that appearances are often deceiving. Jesus warned us that wolves would be walking about in sheep's clothing. Does Mrs. Riplinger qualify for being so? She poses threats to all Christians by lying about her adulteries, and by usurping men's authority in the Church. That's not all. By being an adulteress she teaches although being disqualified making her disorderly. She puts out bad fruit and the sheep have been too sleepy and sheepish to see it. She has been deceitful in covering up her past.

> *"Beware of false prophets, which come to you in sheep's clothing, but inwardly they are ravening wolves."* (Matthew 7:15)

> *"For I know this, that after my departing shall grievous wolves enter in among you, not sparing the flock."* (Acts 20:29)

CHAPTER 5: PHYSICIANS OF NO VALUE

A Phone Call

No matter what one believes about the tragedy of divorce, looking at all sides of the marriages and divorces of Gail Riplinger, the conclusion that must be reached is that the wayward spouse here is Mrs. Gail Riplinger. If she were the innocent one in these failed marriages, it only stands to reason that she would have been more forthright and open about them to all. Instead she chose a dark road of lies and deception. She chose to write a 61 page vicious, vile book listing 13 people she labels as *Traitors.* This book is soundly rebuted by Dr. D.A. Waite in his book, *A Warning! On Gail Riplinger.* Instead of owning up to her guilt and responsibility for her divorces when they were exposed, she reacted with wrath and bitterness. In her book she plays fast and loose with holy scripture, giving out multitudes of verses which being out of context were fired at her targets. This was all intended to make her look like the angel and the 13 defendants appear as devils. Never mind apologizing to the pastors and congregations she lied to and deceived, just kill the messengers.

In case anyone is curious, the people and organizations demonized in her book *Traitors,* is as follows:

MARRIAGE, DIVORCE, & REMARRIAGE

1. Pastor D.A. Waite, Th.D., Ph.D.
2. Mrs. Yvonne Waite
3. D.A. Waite, Jr.
4. Dr. H.D. Williams
5. Dr. Kirk DiVietro
6. Dr. Phil Stringer
7. Dr. Maurice Robinson
8. David W. Cloud
9. Mr. Chris Pinto
10. Dr. Frederick Scrivener
11. Theodore Beza
12. Dr. Robert Barnett
13. The Dean Burgon Society, Incorporated
14. The Bible for Today, Incorporated
15. The Bible for Today Baptist Church[21]

To be very, very clear as to what Mrs. Riplinger is against when attacking people and organizations in "Traitors"; she is against:

1. Those who believe the King James Bible is the only accurate, faithful, and true translation from the Hebrew, Aramaic, and Greek words, but do not believe it is "given by inspiration of God," "inspired by God," "God-breathed," or "inspired in any sense whatever."
2. Those who believe God breathed-out and inspired His words only in Hebrew, Aramaic, and Greek, rather than in

CHAPTER 5: PHYSICIANS OF NO VALUE

English, Spanish, French, Italian, German, Russian, Chinese, Japanese, or in any other language translations made by men.

3. Those who believe that <u>only</u> the original words given by God in Hebrew, Aramaic, and Greek can be called "given by inspiration of God," "inspired of God," "God-breathed," or "inspired" in any sense whatever.[22]

It all started harmless enough. Imagine, the Waites and Mrs. Riplinger considering themselves friends for over ten years. On or about October 24, 2007, Mrs. Yvonne Waite made a phone call to Gail Riplinger. Mrs. Waite asked her about her alleged three marriage and two divorces. Remember, in the 1995 interview Mrs. Waite had with Mrs. Riplinger, no mention of multiple marriages or divorces was made by Mrs. Riplinger. For all the Waites knew up to October of 2007, Mrs. Riplinger and Michael Riplinger were each married for the first time.

In the 2007 phone call the Waites only had hearsay evidence of something fishy. They didn't believe the unfounded rumors and Mrs. Riplinger denied to both Mr. and Mrs. Waite that the rumors were true. She categorically denied them on the phone. She was just married to one man, Michael Riplinger. That is what she said. She was asked the questions in multiple ways, each retorted by Mrs. Riplinger the lie that she had been married only once.

During a Bible conference on January 10-11, 2008 in Princeton, New Jersey, a call came in during the question and answer period. Dr. Waite was asked to comment on the multiple marriage and divorces of Mrs. Riplinger.

Letters, Threats, More Lies

At that Bible conference in January of 2008 at Straightway Baptist Church, Dr. Waite was asked if it was true that Gail Riplinger was divorced. Dr. Waite gave the only response he knew he could at the time; which was that Mrs. Riplinger had denied being previously married twice and previously divorced twice and that she had only been married to Michael Riplinger. Her quote was "had been married to the same man for all these years." Dr. Waite, because of his belief and defense of Mrs. Riplinger's lies, and repeating this again, was held up to mockery on a KJB blog as a defender of lies. On January 11, 2008, on the Bible Versions Discussion Board, the editor called it "Waites historical revisionism."[23]

CHAPTER 5: PHYSICIANS OF NO VALUE

Because of this and testimony of a friend of Dr. Waite, he pursued some further research on the matter. He wrote to the three places in Ohio where the three Riplinger marriages were performed. Dr. Waite received certified copies of Gail Riplinger's three marriages on June 26, June 30, and July 1, 2008, the documented and non-refutable proof of Mrs. Riplinger's three marriages and her intentional deceitful lies and cover up of her fraud was going to be exposed for all to see.

At the annual Dean Burgon Society meeting of July 2008 Dr. Waite exposed the lies of Mrs. Gail Ludwig Latesse Kaleda Riplinger. Here is a list of the documents that Dr. Waite has and the timeline it forms in the matter:

1. July 9-14, 2009 – Mrs. Waite's letter to Gail Riplinger (21 pages)
2. July 21, 2009 – "Bryn A. Riplinger's (Mrs. Shutt) email letter to Dr. and Mrs. Waite (2 pages).
3. August 2009, BFTUPDATE (4 pages)
4. September, October, December 2009 BFTUPDATE (8 pages)
5. November 24, 2009, David Cloud's report on "Gail Riplinger's lies to Dr. and Mrs. D.A. Waite" (3 pages).
6. December 21, 2009, David Cloud's report

on "Gail Riplinger's Lies to the Waites – Part 2 (3 pages).
7. January 4, 2010 – Gail Riplinger's letter to the Waites, threatening to sue me if I didn't retract some things in two weeks (17 pages).
8. About January 10, 2010 – Dr. D.A. Waite's answer to Gail Riplinger's threat to sue him (unpublished) (11 pages).
9. About January 15, 2010 – Dr. Phil Stringer's letter on "Does Dr. Gail Riplinger have a right to sue those who disagree with her?" (4 pages).
10. January 15, 2010 – David Cloud's report on "Gail Riplinger threatens to sue Dr. and Mrs. Waite." (5 pages).
11. February 17, 2010 – "Dr. D.A. Waite's summary of Gail Riplinger and suing Baptists." (2 pages).
12. February 10, 2010 – "Dr. D.A. Waite's summary of Gail Riplinger's 61 page false attack on him, and others." (2 pages).
13. February 17, 2010 – Dr. D. A. Waite's verses pertaining to the following topics: a.) Jezebel, b,) women forbidden to lead men, c.) qualifications for pastors and Christian Leaders, d.) Adultery, e.) wives staying with their husbands, and f.) traitors.[24]

Since Dr. Waite exposed Mrs. Riplinger's three marriages and two divorces at the DBS 31st meeting in Chicago in 2008, Gail Riplinger has been on a tear of anger by first threatening to sue Dr. Waite, Mrs. Waite, and others. When that wasn't going to go anywhere she changed tactics and wrote the 61-page book she entitled, *Traitors.* This is taken apart and the lies proven for what they are in the book by Dr. Waite, *A Warning! On Gail Riplinger's KJB and multiple Inspiration Heresy.*

Beware, those who defend Peter S. Ruckman as a pastor, you're next, also those who defend Gail Riplinger's divorces, when Scripture refutes both. Saints, do not continue to believe in this Jezebel who teaches in your houses of worship. She is not being honest with you, but now has no choice. Her private life has been exposed because God has strict moral guidelines for men for such doings and these equally apply to women. God says teachers must be moral examples and live a pure and honest life. Mrs. Riplinger has done anything but.

Peter S. Ruckman

That name may conjure up a myriad of thoughts, visions, or nightmares. He will be dispensed with in much shorter order than Mrs. Riplinger, for many of the same reasons plus a few others. To be up front, Christians must stop following this man who is and has been for most of his ministry been disqualified. This man believes that the King James Bible was inspired (breathed-out) by God and takes the place of God's own words in the Hebrew and Aramaic and Greek received traditional texts. According to Mr. Ruckman we no longer need the Hebrew, Aramaic, and Greek texts. This person has pitched his nonsense especially against Fundamentalists such as Dr. D.A. Waite. He is to be severely admonished as a brother and pray brothers and sisters God puts it in your heart to not count him as an enemy. The problem is that he will treat everyone as an enemy who disagrees with him. In 1989 he said:

> "The polemics in the publications by Donald Waite...are dedicated to that proposition, and pretense that they are protecting you from heresy is just so much hot air in a wind bag."

So much for the hot air. The bottom line with Ruckman is that you are a *persona non gratis* if you reject Ruckmanism. Ruckmanism is the belief that the King James Bible was given by the inspiration (God-breathed) of God. So, if a Christian Saint just happens to run into Ruckman and disagree on some textual point he opens himself up to being called a "Jackass," "poor, dumb, stupid red legs," "silly asses," "two-bit junkie," "Jacklegs," etc. This is just mean-spirited, fleshly name calling. It doesn't stop there. If you reject him and his strange doctrines then you are a member of a cult, but not just any cult. Read what Ruckman believes:

> "Every recognized church historian and Christian scholar is a member of a cult. This cult is the Alexandrian Cult of North Africa, and its tentacles stretch from Origen (184-254.A.D.) to John R. Rice and the faculty members of every recognized Christian school in the world.[25]

This background for this sort of man leads us into his views to marriage, divorce, and remarriage.

Ruckman and Divorce

Peter Ruckman has been married three times and divorced two times, which makes him remarried two times. This should be enough to see his views on marriage (he takes marriage lightly), divorce (he believes in also) and remarriage (he also believes in). One thing sets him apart from most. He has been a pastor the whole time. He unscripturally defends his unscriptural marital state in his book, *Marriage, Divorce and Remarriage*.

Before he was saved he was in his first

marriage. This was to a woman named Janie M. Their divorce was settled December 20, 1962. Somewhere around that time Sherrell and Ronald Reuban had divorced. Sherrell Reuban then became the second Mrs. Peter S. Ruckman. At this point Peter Ruckman did not meet the divine qualifications for being a pastor set forth by God. Peter Ruckman and his cohort Karl Baker vehemently defend being divorced and in the pastorate in opposition to God's words. Ruckman began pastoring the Brent Baptist Church in Pensacola, Florida shortly after filing for divorce from his first wife Janie. That first marriage ended in violence in which he grabbed Janie by the wrists, and pushed her against a table and a sink, bruising her.[26]

All details about the personal life of Mr. Ruckman have been made available by Ruckman himself in his own publications. His first divorce trial went all the way to the Alabama Supreme Court.

Second Divorce

Peter Ruckman states in his Bible Believers' Bulletin of October 2009 that he became a pastor in 1960 at Brent Baptist Church. He was Pastor of Bible Baptist Church form 1974 to the present. So Ruckman himself proclaims that he has been a pastor continuously for nearly fifty-five years, being divorced twice and married three times.

The second time he was married it was to a young former wife of one of his students[27]. She was divorced.

All the reasons aside, his second marriage in 1972 split the Brent Baptist Church as one-third opposed the marriage.[28]

With seventy-five people he started Bible Baptist Church in Pensacola, FL. This was in 1974. He was divorced for a second time when his wife walked out and sued for a divorce in 1988.

The third marriage is to a member of his own congregation in 1989 to a mother of three.

In Light of God's Words

God's words condemn a man who is not the husband of just one wife, but multiple wives as sinning. It also disqualifies him from serving in the pulpit and preaching God's holy words from it. Peter Ruckman ignores these warnings and sees his path as the right one in his eyes. Trouble is, God sees it differently. Who do we serve, God or ourselves? Peter Ruckman can preach, there's nothing wrong with that. With his two divorces and very chaotic family life he can surely preach in jails, in homes for the elderly and on the streets of Pensacola. Flat out, he should never have preached from the pulpit in any Church.

God's words contain the wisdom of the qualifications for a pastor. Now, Ruckman, Riplinger, Karl Baker, and some others of their ilk, truly despise this teaching by God on the qualifications of a pastor. Contained in the majority of writing and opinions, not only held by scholars and high Church leaders (all cultists to Ruckman), all agree that a divorced man should not occupy the pastorate. They all know that they have the proper interpretation about that from God with nothing private interfering. However, Ruckman and others of his ilk fight with legs and arms kicking wildly about this.

The qualifications of a bishop, pastor, and elder (all the same office), are given by God in 1 Timothy 3:1-7 and Titus: 6-9. 1 Timothy 3:1-7 says:

1. *"This is a true saying, if a man desire the office of a bishop, he desireth a good work.*

2. *A bishop then must be blameless, the husband of one wife, vigilant, sober, of good behaviour, given to hospitality, apt to teach;*

CHAPTER 5: PHYSICIANS OF NO VALUE

3. *Not given to wine, no striker, not greedy of filthy lucre; but patient, not a brawler, not covetous;*

4. *One that ruleth well his own house, having his children in subjection with all gravity;*

5. *For if a man know not how to rule his own house, how shall he take care of the Church of God?*

6. *Not a novice, lest being lifted up with pride he fall into the condemnation of the devil.*

7. *Moreover he must have a good report of them which are without; lest he fall into reproach and the snare of the devil."*

Titus 1:6 says:

"If any be blameless, the husband of one wife, having faithful children not accused of riot or unruly,"

It is the phrase "the husband of one wife" that is tripping up and troubling Mr. Ruckman and those of his ilk. That one little phrase present in 1 Timothy 3:2 and identically repeated in Titus 1:6 is the most controversial and has Dr. Peter Ruckman's entire pastorate hinging upon. However, it is very late now, Ruckman being in his 90's, the damage having been done. But consider that here is one infamous Christian leader who lambasts sound pastors and Christians for being Pharisees when it turns out he is the

King of Pharisees. He has tyrannically manipulated and twisted Scripture to use as a battering ram against the entire Church. It is truly sad.

So this one little twice repeated Greek phrase, *mia gune aner*, the husband of one wife is to be interpreted and understood as Timothy would have when Paul taught him this. It has been problematic for many over the years to understand this properly. We know that we will not get anything but a private and unsound interpretation from Mr. Ruckman. But to a good portion of the Church the phrase means that a bishop must not be a polygamist. This is dismissed as not being common Paul's time. The counter to that is when converts came into the early Church they brought this particular vice with them. Some say there is ample evidence of this. Paul may not have felt it to be the massive problem that some think it is, since he does not distinctly deal with it anywhere in the Scriptures.

These verses do provide the context of what the character makeup of a pastor should be. It can be interpreted as being a one-woman man or a one-wife husband. The Greek construction points to a male who loves only one woman and she being his wife. This holds that the man is a husband married

CHAPTER 5: PHYSICIANS OF NO VALUE

to only one woman at a time. Simply, he cannot be an elder if he has been divorced and remarried, regardless of circumstances, and regardless of whether the marriage happened before he was saved.[29]

He cannot be divorced, remarried, and have a living wife or living wives. If the first and/or second wives die the person can remarry in the Lord. A man who is divorced and remarried, and his first wife is still alive, cannot be a bishop since he would not be the husband of one wife.

It is established that the bishop, pastor, elder must be the husband (a male) with only one living wife (a female).

Now, enter Sir Peter Ruckman. Remember, disagree with him, and you are a member of the Alexandrian Cult! Oh my, lions, and tigers, and bears. Listen to him and his tone on page 25 of his *Marriage, Divorce and Remarriage*:

> "You see, these dumb Fundamentalists --...they're harebrained; they're scatterbrained-they have a persecution complex. They're sensitive; they're touchy; they're emotionally upset; they're disturbed."

The majority of sound Fundamentalists, and other saints who are acquainted with Mr. Ruckman would say he is analyzing himself.

He then goes on to say that we find in 1 Corinthians 7 another ground for divorce: death. That is not a ground for divorce, it breaks the marriage bond according to God.

> *"But if her husband be dead, she is free from that law; so that she is no adulteress, though she be married to another man."* (Romans 7:3b)

She is loosed from that law that bound her to her husband. She is not put away, as Ruckman theorizes, but is free. But we dally in such prattle and must move on to how he really feels in his eyes about being a husband of one wife. It seems that Dr. Ruckman had a discussion with one of the brethren who had received some sound instruction in the word of God about being a husband to one wife. Let's tune in: (this is from Ruckman's own book on marriage, (P26):

He said:

> I believe a bishop is only to have one wife. A man can't be pastor unless he has one wife, and if he has any former wife living anywhere, he has got more than one wife."

Ruckman:

> "Do you really believe that?"

CHAPTER 5: PHYSICIANS OF NO VALUE

(Reminds me of" "yea, hath God said,?" (Genesis 3:1) (author)

He said:

"Yes, I do."

Ruckman:

"In plainer words, you must interpret 1 Timothy 3:2 as the bishop must only be married once, right?"

He said:

"Right."

Ruckman:

"You don't believe that."

He said:

'Sure I do."

Ruckman:

"I'm, going to pin you down. Are you trying to say that being the husband of one wife means that a man, to be a minister (he changes it now), should only have gone through one marriage ceremony with a wedding ring? Is that what you're saying?"

He said:

"Yes, except in the case of death."

Ruckman:

"Hold the phone a minute, man. If the fellow remarried after death, it would be two marriages and two rings and two certificates; you said one."

That is exactly the point. But Ruckman in all his wile does not even see what he said. He tries to bolster his point by twisting Romans 7 by saying it was a woman stepping out on her husband, while he was alive. It has to mean that and be malleable enough to be shaped to Ruckman's preconceived conception of the husband of one wife. If Romans 7 freed the woman from the marriage bond to marry again, and it's true the other way around too, then Ruckman's house of cards would collapse on itself. But don't hold your breath, he will never be able to accept this until he is in the presence of our Lord Jesus Christ.

Getting back to holding the phone, the point is if the pastor-widower would re-marry, the pastor would still be considered "the husband of one wife." Ruckman would be wise to notice: he is the "husband" of a "wife," singular.

There can be only one conclusion to Mr. Ruckman's dilemma. Deep down he may just be hoping and wishing that he was a widower twice over, so that the Scripture could be fulfilled for him.

CHAPTER 6

DIVORCE AND REMARRIAGE

Divorce

"What therefore God hath joined together, let no man put asunder." (Mark 10:9)

The divorce problem does have a notable concern for this author. Being divorced, and the wife being deceased, what the Bible had to say about divorce and remarriage was important. The truth about this subject should be studied thoroughly by every Christian. Prayer must be applied to seek the courage to face and understand God's truth about divorce and remarriage.

Do we allow only what the Scriptures allow or do we allow lowering the standards that permit for "every cause" divorce?

Is divorce dissolution to marriage? Is there divorce for adultery, and if there is does that leave any question as to remarriage? If there is no divorce for adultery, then there has to be no remarriage.

If dissolution is achieved by divorce, and divorce due to an adulterous mate, then there must be remarriage based on dissolution. Remarriage must be denied by proving grounds of non-dissolution of divorce for any reason.

The ancient Jews allowed for divorce and remarriage for every cause. It is much the same in the United States with thirty or more grounds for divorce accepted. In Old Testament times, before the Captivity, many wives and many concubines made for polygamous marriages.

By the time Jesus came a man could only have one wife, but many were divorced for every cause and remarried. When Jesus came along He restricted divorce to one reason and one reason only. There are those who say that is not true. If Jesus allowed divorce for the cause of all sexual sin and allowed remarriage for the innocent party, this was still small consolation for the Jews compared to what they were used to. It is no wonder they rejected the authority of Christ and continued to walk according to their own way. Or did the Jews and the rest of the Gentile world miss the point. Did Jesus not ban all divorce and subsequent remarriage?

No one person, lay or clergy, has either the time or the resources for a complete and comprehensive study on the subject of divorce and remarriage.

The Early Church and Church Fathers

From the outset of the early Church it was obvious how divorce and remarriage was received. For the first 500 years after Christ any remarriage after divorce for any reason was considered adulterous. The marriage was for life and if adultery occurred it was understood the other spouse was to separate but not remarry. Jewish and Roman law gave more freedom to the man and not the woman in a marriage. If the woman had the affair that was adultery, but if the man was guilty of a dalliance that was fornication. Polygamy was okay for Jews and Roman men had their concubines along with a wife. The early Christians taught equity in a marriage on matters of sex and each other. Paul taught the ownership of each other's bodies and this figured into the equity equation. There was to be complete faithfulness between Christian spouses and this was reflected in the Father's refusal to approve of remarriage after divorce.

Hermas

Hermas, a resident of Rome wrote the work, *The Shepherd of Hermas,* somewhere between 100 and 150 A.D. Even this date is questioned by J.T. Robinson who dates it at no later than 85 A.D. This is the earliest known Christian teaching on the subject of divorce and was held in high regard by Irenaeus, Clement of Alexandria, Tertullian, and Athanasius.

In the dialogue he has with a heavenly guardian the question is raised if a husband could continue living with a persistently adulterous wife after he becomes aware of that situation. What should the man do if he finds he is partner to a wife who is an adulterer? To avoid becoming guilty of her sin he would be instructed to send her away and remain single. If he were to remarry that would make him guilty of adultery. However, by remaining single leaves open the possibility of the wife repenting and returning to her husband. By forbidding remarriage and making it a responsibility to receive again a repentant wife, Hermas was in opposition to the Civil Law of Rome at that time. This seems to coincide with Paul's teaching on 1 Corinthians 7:11 "But and if she depart, let her remain unmarried, or be reconciled to her husband: and let not the husband put away his wife."

So, Hermas believed what the early Christians believed about marriage and divorce. First, a separated husband must not

CHAPTER 6: DIVORCE & REMARRIAGE

remarry but remain single; second, if the adulterous wife repents she must be taken back; and third, these principles would apply to a separated wife and an adulterous husband.

Justin Martyr

Justin Martyr was a second century Christian apologist born around 100 A.D., though the date of his birth is unknown. He was born to and brought up by Greek parents and was very much into philosophies of the times looking for answers to life. He opened a Christian school of philosophy, mixed philosophy with the Christian faith, but ended up defending the Christian faith for which he was martyred by beheading by Rome.

He is survived by three of his writings: *First Apology, The Second Apology, and Dialogue With Trypho the Jew*. In the first Apology he quotes Scriptures in Matthew and Luke and follows with the quote, "those who, according to human law, contract double marriages, are sinners against our Master."[1]

What he is saying is that someone who remarries is considered twice married, or a bigamist, in God's eyes and that is a sin. By the divorce being accepted by human laws makes it accepted but it is not accepted by

God. It seems as though Martyr makes a strong case for no remarriage after divorce and possibly no remarriage of any kind. Martyr was clear about Jesus condemning the man who is an adulterer but agrees with our Lord about lusting in our hearts to commit adultery with women. Although the society ruled by Rome around Justin Martyr's time legally recognized remarriage after divorce, he took a stance opposed to the Government of no remarriage after divorce.

Justin Martyr also agrees with Hermas and the Christian belief of his time that a woman had the right to separate from an adulterous husband so as to not partake in any way of their sin.

Tertullian

Tertullian was a second century theologian. He wrote as a private individual in most of his early works, but in *De Momogamia,* (207 A.D.) he wrote representing a group, expounding sectarian dogma.[2]

Tertullian was a Montanist and as one maintained the continuance of the marriage bond after the death of one of the spouses in defiance of what Paul taught in Romans 7:

> "but if her husband be dead, she is free from that law;"

CHAPTER 6: DIVORCE & REMARRIAGE

We can conclude that Tertullian believed in marriage as being between one man and one woman and one marriage only.

He stated in *De Monogamia*:

> "...the Paraclete (Holy Ghost) could have forbidden marriage altogether, much more had he to proclaim against remarriage,... that the discipline of monogamy (he defines as the right to marry only once), is nothing new nor a thing imported into Christianity,"[3]

An interesting observation into Tertullian that applies to being a priest, or by extension a Pastor, "Do you offer, do you baptize, being a digamist? (defined as a widower who has married again).[4]

He did not believe this way before he became a Montanist. In fact, he criticized and was a most vociferous opponent of Montanism. However, he joined the Montanist Community of Carthage. Montanism followed the strict teachings of Montanus of Phrygia in Asia Minor. He self-declared himself a prophet and said the age of the Holy Spirit and the end of the world was near. It was through Montanus that Tertullian taught that a second marriage after the death of a spouse was forbidden. The Council of Constantinople condemned Montanism in 381 A.D. but the movement prevailed finally dying out in the 6th Century. All the heretical doctrines of the Montanists did was to corrupt the Christian doctrines of the Holy Spirit and eschatology which Tertullian bought into.

To Rome

It may be interesting to read about and study about the Church Fathers and what they had to say about Christian doctrine, but the fact is the "Fathers" were mostly heretics and held many heretical positions. On marriage, divorce, and remarriage though they mostly agreed with the Apostles and early Church and carried on that tradition. If a roll call of the best known early Christian theologian "Fathers" was taken it would be found that nearly all of them upheld the tradition that remarriage after divorce was contrary to the Scriptures. In H. Crouzel's monumental work, *L'eglise face au divorce* (1971) all the relevant texts have been exhaustively and carefully studied.[5]

Crouzel found only one exception in all his studies. That one exception was someone named Ambrosiaster, who was mistakenly identified as Bishop Ambrose of Milan, did approve of remarriage after some divorces. That allowance was for a deserted, innocent husband which he didn't extend to

CHAPTER 6: DIVORCE & REMARRIAGE

a woman suffering the same plight.

Suffice it to say that the earliest Church was very concerned about the spiritual health of the Church and the community. Hence, they sought to deal decisively with those who would justify any position on divorce and remarriage contrary to the Scriptures, in favor of repentance and repair of damaged marriages. There was clarity and unity in the Church with regards to upholding the teachings of Christ on divorce and remarriage. It is a lesson to the Modern Church of discipline in the expression of the Lord's love for sinners.

We have discussed earlier some of the teachings of Jesus on divorce. In Deuteronomy 24:1-4 it was commanded that a man had to write a legal paper called a "bill of divorcement" to his wife if he was to put her away or divorce her. When Jesus walked on the earth two schools of thought fought for their meaning of the term "uncleanness" to prevail on when divorce would be acceptable in God's eyes.

The school of Shammai allowed divorce only for the sin of adultery, and was seen as being too strict for the people then. The liberal school of Hillel considered any infraction or lesser irritation to the husband as being grounds for divorce. Therefore, the question of the Pharisees was put to Jesus if it was lawful to divorce for every cause. This question was being asked in the liberal context which was supported by most of the Jewish people.

The difficulty arises when pastors, deacons, and all others in the Church, including the influential scholars agree that Jesus disallowed all divorce and right to remarry, and run into the interpretation wall of the Matthean exception clauses. The clear view of the clauses according to the early Church would be bestowing grounds for separation only with the only options of repentance and reconciliation or the singleness of both parties as long as they would live.

Erasmus + Protestant Tradition

The earliest Christian position on divorce and remarriage held firm from the time of Jesus until the early sixteenth century when Erasmus presented his idea which has influenced Protestant, Evangelical and New Evangelical thought ever since. During the Reformation Protestant theologians who followed Luther merely extended their arguments built upon those first set forth by Erasmus.

CHAPTER 6: DIVORCE & REMARRIAGE

Roman Catholic Interuptus

The Roman Catholic interpretation of marriage as a sacrament started with Augustine. He denied remarriage to all, including the so-called innocent party after a divorce. Marriage to him was a mystery, nearly mystical in its sacramental union of Christ and the Church. He applied Ephesians 5:31-32 to mean the joining of the Church to Christ in a mystical, sacramental way. Paul was talking about the joining of the husband and wife as forming one flesh and thus being joined spiritually with Christ. Augustine put forth the proposition that the joining was symbolic and merely alluded to as an analogy of Christ's unity with the Church. Luther also believed it to be only a symbolic unity.

Thomas Aquinas came along and furthered the Romanist view that grace was derived from the sacramental act of marrying two people and as being on a par with the Catholic's other six sacraments which include: baptism, confirmation, the Eucharist, penance, extreme unction, and holy orders. Thus, the distorting of the Scripture continued: "For this cause shall a man leave his father and mother, and shall be joined unto his wife, and they two shall be one flesh.

This is a great mystery: but I speak concerning Christ and the church." (Ephesians 5:31-32)

The Council of Trent soundly affirmed this notion that the marriage sacrament was one of many instruments that God has at His disposal to inject supernatural grace into the very souls of a married couple. This is the foundation of the meaning of marriage as a sacrament for the Catholic Church up to this day.

It was Erasmus who reacted to the Romish misinterpretation of Scripture concerning supernatural grace to Roman Catholics by sacrament. When he wrote his Greek Scriptures, in the annotations of his first two editions he discarded the Church's (Roman Catholic) statements about "Sacramentum." He knew from the Greek that it does not actually mean a sacrament but means hidden and secret.

Luther came along and used the Erasmian Texts to refute the sacramental system of Rome as extra-biblical, and scolds them for not having read the Greek for the correct interpretation. Although the Catholic Church was adamant on the indissolubility of the marriage bond, two methods of divorce were and are condoned. One was a separation from bed and board, supported by

Augustine and Jerome.[6]

The second method was annulment of the marriage, ending it completely for any one of eighteen reasons. Erasmus was deeply affected by this action of the Roman Church for its opposition to the Scriptures as well as for the abuse it engendered. Erasmus saw that Christ's words deny any form of divorce, yet he sought to use canonical laws to authorize divorce by having them prove a marriage to be illegal from the start. He hoped that his interpretation of the divorce texts would create a higher moral standard for marriage in the Roman Church and later for the believers' Church.

The Erasmian View

In Erasmus's heart, he was helping those who hold to a pure and sound judgment in the Church. He wanted to allow some concessions to those whose opinions were swayed away from no remarriage after divorce for adultery. Thus, he wanted to exegete the verses containing the escape (exception) clauses as granting first the divorce and then remarriage for those considering themselves as the innocent party. Therefore, he backed two enlightened propositions that divorce should be permissible for certain marriages for serious, legitimate reasons, and that the party innocent of adultery would be allowed to remarry. These two views were considered revolutionary and heretical by the theologians of his day.[7]

It was the view of Erasmus that rules for divorce were outside the realm of Christian fundamentals and, therefore, he applied the new thought of the times and surmised that those rules would change as the times and necessity would require. Erasmus had a salvific context in which he sought to justify divorce and remarriage. If things could be done in a charitable way, and allowing divorce and remarriage would relieve suffering, it needed to be allowed and to be done. Erasmus believed that it was Christ that authorized divorce for the cause of adultery only. He also believed Pauline theology expanded the precept of divorce.

The interpretation of Erasmus concerning divorce is mostly identical with modern Christianity today. It is wrongly noted that Erasmus got his nomenclature on the divorce texts by agreeing with and promoting the ideas of Origen. However, Origen said that a man who is married again while a former spouse lives commits adultery. This is not what Erasmus believed. Origen's beliefs included equal conjugal

CHAPTER 6: DIVORCE & REMARRIAGE

rights for the man and woman, and that it was adulterous for a divorced woman to remarry. He never discussed, in relation to Matthew 19, any case of a non-adulterous husband separating from an adulterous wife. Finally, Origen held that non-adulterous spouses could not remarry.

What exactly is an innocent party when divorce is discussed? The innocent party has been given the designation in our day to the spouse that is not guilty of adultery. This is an evangelical positon that assumes the interpretation that Christ allowed divorce for the exception of adultery as found in Matthew 5:32 and Matthew 19:9. If both spouses are guilty of adultery then there is no innocent party. If one person is cleansed by the blood of Christ and is forgiven but the other party continues to live in adultery, then there is an innocent party and in these post-modern, post-Christian times, a possibility for the ending of the marriage. Working to save a marriage is preferred and divorce is never demanded, never required in Scripture, according to them.

Erasmus favored separation of an innocent party from an adulterous spouse and supported remarriage. It was in his nature to help the so-called innocent spouse by allowing remarriage to restore the privileges of the marital relationship. He admits to the difficulty of Matthew 5:32 and 19:9 providing for separation only and not for divorce. He was open to any and all interpretations allowing divorce and remarriage based on the exception clauses.

The interpretation applied to Paul's message in 1 Corinthians 7 was that Christians were under the Gospel and not the law. This freed up many variations for the allowance of divorce and remarriage. Christians were married to Christ so the law no longer had any influence on the Children of God. Erasmus, therefore, misunderstands the absolute Law of God as Paul is stating it in Romans 7:1-3. He calls it a parable of Paul and, therefore, as a parable it does not fit every situation. This is odd since Erasmus believed that Paul in Romans 7:1-3 is not teaching anything about divorce or remarriage. He thought Paul was referring to Deuteronomy 24:1 which breaks the bond of marriage by divorcement, but Paul is saying the law is what binds a man and a woman together until death. To extend further, Erasmus also believes that 1 Corinthians 7:39 was only about teaching on virgins and widows. There was a problem with accepting death as the only breakage of the marital bond.

The Results

The ideas that Erasmus stated started the Protestant Reformers to break from their Roman Catholic roots and also to liberalize their views on divorce and remarriage. The Reformers adopted Erasmus's interpretation of the divorce texts and they stubbornly defended his exegesis from the time they started to circulate. The immediate result of the Erasmian view was that Luther, a Reformation leader, favored the remarriage of the innocent party in the cases of adultery and desertion. But Luther expanded on that and later allowed divorce for more than the reason of adultery.

The results of the early exponents of divorce and remarriage had the direct bearing on what the post-modern evangelical consensus is today. One of the major problems was the misinterpretation of Deuteronomy 24:1-4 and its relation to Christ's teaching in the New Testament divorce texts. The action of *porneia* in the Matthean escape clauses was morally equivalent to "some uncleanness" in Deuteronomy 24:1. The truth was it was for most any reason that a Jewish man could divorce his Jewish wife. The Jewish man would find no favor in his wife and if it turned to hate he would just write a bill of divorcement and send her away. This only confused the issue by saying that "some uncleanness" was adultery. This idea carries over to today.

The Reformers also indulged in the idea that the proven adulterer in a failed marriage should be regarded as if he/she were dead. It was believed during Reformation times that since the Jews stopped the death sentence for adultery, that Christ included the exception clauses in Matthew. The Reformers believed that Christ licensed divorce as a logical progression from the Old to the New Testaments without the death of the adulterer. They mostly disregarded the higher standards that Christ intended such as repentance and reconciliation. The teaching of Genesis 2:24 of one flesh should have prevailed in Reformation thought about the indissolubility of the marriage bond instead of the increasing liberality of divorce rules from Reformer to Reformer.

Another misinterpretation of clear Scripture is the Reformers' view of 1 Corinthians 7:15 which says: "But if the unbelieving depart, let him depart. A brother or a sister is not under bondage in such cases:" The Reformers in general take that as bolstering their own view that Jesus was

CHAPTER 6: DIVORCE & REMARRIAGE

saying that adultery was not the only exception permitting divorce and remarriage. Calvin seconded this and as evidence today we find that Bullinger, Bucer, and Peter Martyr use 1 Corinthians 7:15 as their proof verse also to expand divorce allowances beyond adultery. The unity of the early Church's view of divorce and remarriage as being adulterous has given way to the Reformation theology, permitting divorce and remarriage for adultery as well as for other serious grounds.

The Reformers' application of Romans 7:2-5 to the widow remarrying in good conscience signals a further move away from traditional teaching. Christ's teaching that, "what therefore God hath joined together, let no man put asunder" (Matthew 19:6) gives way to the Reformed refrain of not applying to divorce by adultery because, "the law of capital punishment and Christ's exception make God, and not man, the author of divorce for adultery." [8]

The early Church held faithfully to Matthew 19:6 and Mark 10:9 as meaning that a man and a wife, joined together by God was to become an indissoluble union broken only by the death of one of the spouses.

Erasmian Camps

As stated before, the views of Erasmus regarding divorce and remarriage influenced the Reformers and have blossomed into the Church's confusion today. Beth and Wenham in their book, *Jesus and Divorce,* list three camps.

1. The first one says only adultery or desertion justifies full divorce with the right to remarriage.
2. The second camp believes that *porneia,* (fornication, uncleanness, or unchastity) is a wider term than adultery and that Matthew 19:9 permits divorce and remarriage for a wide range of sins.
3. The third says that the Matthean exception clauses that permit remarriage after divorce was not the original intent of Jesus. Jesus taught the indissolubility of marriage and that Matthew changed Christ's teaching to allow divorce in some hard cases.

John and Paul Feinberg, in *Ethics for a Brave New World,* categorize three Evangelical groups:

1. There are no grounds for divorce or remarriage. Marriage is a covenant and cannot be broken. The so-called exception clauses in Matthew were not

CHAPTER 6: DIVORCE & REMARRIAGE

referring to divorce but to an annulment for fornication before marriage.
2. Divorce is permissible, but remarriage is not. The Scriptures allow for divorce for adultery and desertion by an unbelieving spouse, but no allowance for remarriage. Death of a spouse is the only clear scriptural allowance for remarriage. This view allows for the "Pauline Privilege" in 1 Corinthians 7 of divorce in the cases of cases of abandonment and *porneia*, but allows for no remarriage.
3. The third view permits divorce and/or remarriage for adultery and/or desertion. There are many variations but accept the Matthean exception clauses allowing divorce and biblical support for divorce and remarriage for the innocent party in cases of sexual immorality and/or abandonment.

Andreas J. Kostenberger categorizes four distinct Evangelical views on divorce and remarriage:

1. The first view espouses the biblical legitimacy of divorce and remarriage for the innocent party of a spouse's adultery/sexual immorality and of an unbelieving spouse's desertion.
2. The second view holds to divorce for adultery and an unbelieving spouse's

desertion but not remarriage.
3. The third view allows for neither divorce nor remarriage in the case of adultery and for divorce but not for remarriage in the case of desertion by an unbelieving spouse.
4. The fourth and final position is that no divorce or remarriage for adultery but divorce and remarriage in the case of desertion by an unbeliever.

Divorce Prohibited

"Yet ye say, wherefore? Because the Lord hath been witness between thee and the wife of thy youth, against whom thou hast dealt treacherously: yet is she thy companion, and the wife of thy covenant.

...therefore take heed to your spirit, and let none deal treacherously against the wife of his youth. For the Lord, the God of Israel, saith that he hateth putting away:" (Malachi 2:14, 15b, 16a)

We as Christians should hate divorce because God hates divorce (He hateth putting away). Christians should love those who are divorced because God loves them. The practice of divorce should be discouraged in the strongest way possible since God calls it violent and treacherous. The Bible should be the standard for

CHAPTER 6: DIVORCE & REMARRIAGE

marriage and divorce should never be encouraged in the Church. Preachers must stand strong in the word to turn away the tide that favors divorce and remarriage.

Clear Scriptures

"And he saith unto them, whosoever shall put away his wife, and marry another, committeth adultery against her."

"And if a woman shall put away her husband, and be married to another, she committeth adultery." (Mark 10: 11,12)

"Whosoever putteth away his wife, and marrieth another, committeth adultery: and whosoever marrieth her that is put away from her husband committeth adultery." (Luke 16:18)

"For the woman which hath an husband is bound by the law to her husband so long as he liveth; but if the husband be dead, she is loosed from the law of her husband.."

"So then if, while her husband liveth, she be married to another man, she shall be called an adulteress: but if her husband be dead, she is free from that law; so that she is no adulteress, though she be married to another man." (Romans 7:2-3)

"The wife is bound by the law as long as her husband liveth; but if her husband be dead, she is at liberty to be married to

> whom she will; only in the Lord. (1 Corinthians 7:39)

The prohibition of divorce began in Malachi as part of the many things God was severely dealing with Israel about. They would not listen then and not many Christians and Jews are listening now. God means what He says, He is merciful, but there comes a time that He must judge. These four clear Scriptures on divorce leave no room for Evangelical man to be fast and loose with God's words. This is a result of the liberalization in the name of compassion that was started by Erasmus. God says in His words that there is no divorce, period!

Exception clauses?

> *"It hath been said, whosoever shall put away his wife, let him give her a writing of divorcement: But I say unto you, that whosoever shall put away his wife, saving for the cause of fornication, causeth her to commit adultery: and whosoever shall marry her that is divorced committeth adultery:* (Matthew 5:31-32)

> *"And I say unto you, whosoever shall put away his wife, except it be for fornication, and shall marry another, committeth adultery: and whoso marrieth her which is put away doth commit adultery."* (Matthew 19:9)

CHAPTER 6: DIVORCE & REMARRIAGE

These two passages in Scripture, spoken by Jesus, differ from those on divorce that we find in Mark, Luke, and in 1 Corinthians of Paul. There is no contradiction in God's words. The reasons for that are simple and easy to understand. The Gospel of Mark was written for a Gentile audience living in Rome. There are a large amount of Latin terms found in Mark's Gospel.[9]

Luke, in his Gospel wrote to a Greek audience. Paul addressed Romans in his book to the Romans. The Corinthians were mainly Greeks that he wrote to in his epistles.

So, these two passages in Matthew were written primarily to the Jews with references therein that are different than all of the rest of New Testament references. The misunderstanding about the exception clauses found in Matthew exists in the Church today due to the lack of betrothal. Infidelity to one's fiancé (a man engaged to be married) during the betrothal period gave the faithful fiancé the duty to write a bill of divorcement to end the relationship. Thus, the attention Matthew gives to uniquely Jewish concerns should give pause to the Church to reverse themselves on the faulty theology they base their decisions upon. Back before the times of Erasmus, consider the horrific mistakes in exegesis that have been made concerning the Matthean exception and right the wrong.

Betrothal Redux

Although previously explained, more can be added to this Jewish practice. When a young Jewish man wanted to marry a young girl, their parents would decide if it was in their interest for the two to tie the knot. A ceremony was started where a payment was made and certain documents were signed. The betrothal period was begun with the two bound together as in marriage. They were not permitted to have any sex during this one year period. A public wedding was planned for the end of the one year bethrothal period. Jewish Law considered the two married, though limited by restrictions by law.

In the eyes of the Jews fornication, *porneia* and adultery, *moichao* were different sins. Adultery, according to Jewish society, was the sin by the unfaithful partner, or both partners, after consummation of the marriage and after the betrothal period. A partner who had sexual relations outside of the betrothal union and during the betrothal period, committed fornication not adultery. Divorce by a written bill of divorcement was

CHAPTER 6: DIVORCE & REMARRIAGE

only allowed for sexual infidelity during the betrothal period. This was the only divorce or putting away that Christ was talking about and it was very familiar to the Jews by Jewish Laws of marriage and divorce.

We find support for the betrothal view in Matthew's account of Joseph's and Mary's betrothal in Matthew 1:18-25. During the period of engagement, *"his mother Mary was espoused to Joseph"* (V18). This is a separate period from the time that the husband takes the wife into his father's home to consummate the marriage. (Deuteronomy 20:7) *"Before they came together,"* (Matthew 1:18) shows a separate time of consummation after the betrothal.

Critics of this view attempt to not limit *porneia*, the sexual relations of a betrothed person with someone other than his or her betrothed during the time of betrothal. Brug complains, citing an article in the January-March 2008 issue of "Bibliotheca Sacra":

> This view claims that the dissolution of the betrothal in such a case would not really be a divorce leading to remarriage, since it would be an annulment that was never consummated. Thus the "exception clause" would not really be allowing an exception to the rule "no divorce and remarriage."

Berg disagrees with this, as do mostly

all Evangelicals of our post-modern era, arguing that you cannot limit the word *porneia* to sexual relations of one party during betrothal.

David Jones in his paper, "The Betrothal View" states that the view of betrothal;

> "Holds that the exception clause used by Jesus was referring to the unique Jewish practice that allowed for a marriage to be annulled of evidence of infidelity was manifest during the betrothal period. He also states that the Bible prohibits marriage partners from actively seeking divorce, since the exception clause refers to a nuptial custom not followed today."[10]

It can be concluded that Brug and the other Post-Modernists are generating their interpretation of the exception clause themselves independently.

> "Know this first, that no prophecy of the Scriptures is of any private interpretation." (2 Peter 2:20).

The Nature of John 8:41

Many advocates against betrothal as the definitive explanation of the exception clause, also trip up at their own private interpretation of John 8:41. Some miss this verse altogether. Instead of learning that the supposed sin of Mary and Joseph was

CHAPTER 6: DIVORCE & REMARRIAGE

fornication and not adultery, they intermingle the two terms to mean the same thing. This is just not logical on its face, since Jesus would not use both terms if only the one was needed.

Jesus had just finished telling the Pharisees that they should be doing the works of the Father if they truly believed they were following Abraham. They were turning very hostile and threatening Jesus' life. Jesus said, "Ye do the deeds of your father," (John 8:41a), which they instinctively understood Jesus to mean their father was the devil. They shot back the ad hominem attack, *"we be not born of fornication;"* (John 8:41). They were not standing for Jesus' talk since they were accusing him of being born of fornication or illegitimately according to Jewish law.

Heth and Wenham doubt that this can be used as support for fornication making a marriage illegitimate during betrothal.

> "But that John 8:41 can be cited as support for the use of the word porneia as a technical term for unchastity during the betrothal period is doubtful."[11]

The point is that fornication *porneia* and adultery *moichea* are not terms with the same meanings, in ancient times or now. A betrothal could only be broken by a divorce for which the only grounds were if a partner had committed fornication. If there was a putting away of a partner during the betrothal period and there was no fornication committed and it was followed by a marriage, this would constitute adultery. This is why fornication, *porneia* and adultery, *moichea* are used in the same verse.

These two terms are two different Greek words with separate meanings. They are not identical terms with the same identical meanings as many teachers and pastors teach.

Sins are being categorized in Matthew 15:19 separately as fornication and adultery and again in Galatians 5:19, not as the same or we would only need one word to describe the actions. When we read the Bible, fornication always refers to sexual sin committed by a single (engaged or betrothed included) person and adultery refers to sexual sin committed by those who are married.[12]

What Jesus is teaching in Matthew by including the exception for fornication is not contradicted by verses in Mark, Luke, Romans, or 1 Corinthians. This teaching was reinforcing Jewish Law to Jewish people who were being misled by their religious leaders.

CHAPTER 6: DIVORCE & REMARRIAGE

The Rule of Last Mention

W. Fisher-Hunter has written an interesting treatise on the subject of divorce called *The Divorce problem.* In the forward by Professor H.L. Ellison of London, England, he states that it was the result of the flood of heathen into the Western Church that divorce was permitted. He rightly states that the Church of Rome could not square itself with the New Testament teachings of Christ forbidding divorce and remarriage.

Along with re-emphasizing the law of interpretation, that says never to use a doubtful passage of Scripture to contradict a clear positive one, he puts forth another. "And let not the husband put away his wife" (1 Corinthians 7:11) he postulates are the last words in the progressive revelation of the truth of divorce. He states that the rule of last mention as the last part of the revelation of a truth always supercedes in its application the former parts which belong to and have their application in another dispensation.[13]

Hunter uses as an example of this law of the progression of the revelation of truth in the Biblical accounts of the eating of meats. It was before Noah's flood that God had sanctioned only the eating of herbs and vegetables. Genesis 9:3 granted Noah and the rest of mankind the eating of animals together with plants and vegetables. After Israel was formed as a nation God separated the clean from the unclean animals for the Israelites to eat. To Peter in Acts 10 God, "Cleansed, that call not thou common." After the church was instituted and empowered, God removed all restrictions that had been placed by Moses on the eating of meats. (As per Paul's instructions to the Christians in Romans 14:1-15; to Timothy in 1 Tim. 4:3-5; and Peter's vision in Acts 11:5-9)[14]

The progression for meats therefore throughout the dispensations starting before the flood was that only herbs and vegetables were allowed up to the flood. After the flood meat was permitted for Noah and limited to Israel after they became a nation. For Christians the restrictions of clean and unclean animals were lifted and all meats are clean and edible to him.

The progressive revelation of the truth of divorce and according to the rule of last mention is as follows:

1.) Divorce was first legalized and circumscribed by Moses and permitted to the male sex only in Israel (Deut. 24:1,2). 2.) The Lord Jesus allowed the privilege as originally prescribed to remain in force to men in Israel, (Matt. 5:32; 19:9). 3.) The Lord when speaking on divorce privately to his disciples made no allowance for it, and branded as an adulterer the divorced person who remarries (Mark 10: 11,12), and 4.) Sixty years after the legal, ceremonial, and judicial enactments of the Law of Moses had been absolutely abrogated for the Christian (Romans 7: 3,4), Paul gives the Lord's commandment for the Churches on divorce which is as follows: "Unto the married I command, yet not I, but the Lord, let not the wife depart from her husband: But and if she depart, let her remain unmarried, or be reconciled to her husband: and let not the husband put away his wife." (1 Corinthians 7: 10,11).

If the Scriptures are not reconciled and understood according to the dispensations, confusion and misunderstanding will occur. There is ample evidence of this very fact all throughout the Church. A Christian should easily understand that the teaching of Moses on divorce is different than the Lord's teaching to his Disciples and the Church. Rather than realizing that these divorce texts do not contradict each other, as a lot of Church leaders teach today to the contrary, the simple truth on divorce need only be understood as belonging to different dispensations.[15]

Deuteronomy 24:1,2; Matthew 5:32 and 19:9 are for the Jew under the Law of Moses. Mark 10: 11, 12; Luke 16:18; and 1 Corinthians 7:10,11 are for the Lord's people in this present dispensation of grace. When applying the Rule of Last Mention of God's words on marital separation, divorce and remarriage for God's people today it is found in First Corinthians 7: 10-17.[16]

Against Remarriage

> *"And whoso marrieth her which is put away doth commit adultery."* (Matthew 19: 9b)

This part of the divorce text spoken by Jesus does not allow for remarriage for one that is put away. If it is understood that Jesus was allowing for divorce for sexual sin after marriage, 19:9b negates that. The divorce texts do not allow for remarriage for any spouse, except for the death of one of the spouses.

> *"But if the unbelieving depart, let him depart. A brother or a sister is not under bondage in such cases:"* (1 Corinthians 7:15)

This verse is used by those who believe that Matthew approved divorce and that remarriage is now in order. This particular verse is not giving divorcees permission to

CHAPTER 6: DIVORCE & REMARRIAGE

remarry. Paul has already stated that this is true.

> *"And unto the married I command, yet not I, but he Lord, let not the wife depart from her husband: but and if she depart, let her remain unmarried, or be reconciled to her husband: and let not the husband put away his wife."* (1 Corinthians 7:10,11)

The husband is not to put away his wife and leave the marriage. Next, Paul speaks to spiritually mixed marriages where one of the two spouses has become saved somewhere along in the marriage. Paul commands what the Lord wants for these types of marriages. The believing husband is commanded to not divorce the unbelieving wife. He commands a believing wife not to leave the unsaved husband. A Christian's duty is to live with an unsaved partner for that partner's sake for the believer to have his/her influence on the unsaved spouse and to raise the children as believers. With prayer and perseverance the unsaved may come to believe in Christ and be saved.

In reference to 1 Corinthians 7:15 and the departure of the unbeliever this verse says that God is not holding the believer responsible for preserving the marriage union. That means the believer need not fight divorce actions coming from the unbeliever. Legally it is not necessary to employ tactics to prevent these actions since God "hath called us to peace." This may end up for a believer being no longer bound to their spouse in marriage, the law of God is still in effect for the believer. The deserted believer is free from the marriage but verse 15 does not teach anything about the freedom to remarry. According to 1 Corinthians 7:11 there are only two alternatives that God allows: reconcile with the separated partner, or to live the rest of his/her life being single as long as the other spouse is alive.

Some Reasons Not to Divorce and Remarry

1. God first instituted marriage between a man and a woman. Divorce was not in view at all.

> "Therefore shall a man leave his father and mother and shall cleave unto his wife: and they shall be one flesh." (Genesis 2:24)

2. God hates divorce.

> "For the Lord, the God of Israel, saith that he hateth putting away: for one covereth violence with his garment, saith the Lord of hosts: therefore, take heed to your spirit, that ye deal not treacherously." (Malachi 2:16).

CHAPTER 6: DIVORCE & REMARRIAGE

God calls divorce violence and treachery.

3. Marriage originally ordained by God is binding and does not permit polygamy, divorce or remarriage of divorced persons.

> *"What therefore God hath joined together, let no man put asunder."* (Mark 10:9)

> *"Whosoever shall put away his wife, and marry another, committeth adultery against her. And if a woman shall put away her husband, and be married to another, she committeth adultery."* (Mark 10:11,12).

4. Moses when he permitted divorcement for the men of Israel, never legislated for the Church. The Lord Jesus further allowed divorce for Jewish men under the law who were not his disciples.

5. The Lord Jesus did not permit his own disciples privately for any divorce, labeling as an adulterer a divorced person who remarries.

6. The Lord's own prohibition against divorce and remarriage.

> *"Wherefore they are no more twain, but one flesh. What therefore God hath*

MARRIAGE, DIVORCE, & REMARRIAGE

joined together, let not man put asunder." (Matthew 19:6)

"But and if she depart, let her remain unmarried, or be reconciled to her husband: and let not the husband put away his wife." (1 Corinthains 7:11)

7. Christians are prohibited from taking another Christian to a worldly court, the only way to obtain a legal divorce.

"Dare any of you, having a matter against another, go to law before the unjust, and not before the saints?" (1 Corinthians 6:1)

CHAPTER 7

HOMOSEXUALITY AND MARRIAGE

Introduction

> *"If a man also lie with mankind, as he lieth with a woman, both of them have committed an abomination:"* (Leviticus: 20:13a).

The homosexual lifestyle is here with us. God told Christians that it would be so. The homosexual has imposed an immoral lifestyle upon mainstream culture and everything is fine and dandy in their eyes.

> *"...but every man did that which was right in his own eyes."* (Deuteronomy 17:6b)

If you listen to them there is nothing in the Bible that God says about them. They can rationalize and explain away any condemnation that anyone in Jesus name would wish to bring before them. Part of that is the hardness of their hearts from turning away from God. They have set the stage for their very scary lifestyle. They are in our schools with an agenda portraying homosexuals as victims of society. The day of silence observed every year teaches young minds to be tolerant and for any LGBT kids present, to feel good about themselves. Now if you question the lifestyle of the gays you are attacked for being intolerant, unaccepting, and a homophobe. The TV is now flooded with the gay lifestyle as well as homosexual news and movies.

It took many strides to get to this point. The commitment factor within straight marriages was weakening starting in the 60s. More liberal divorce laws made it easier to dissolve marriages. Temporary relationships outside of marriage flourished and were fueled by the media depicting marriage as tedious and the opposite of fun. In 1973 the Association of American Psychiatrists (AAP) classified homosexuality as normal. More and more homosexuals were revealing themselves as gay and were more accepted and not considered criminal. Same-sex couples pushed the agenda for unions that were recognized by the states as legal. It has been the courts of the land that have made all these changes possible.

Finally it came down to same-sex marriage being decided in the courts to determine if the Constitution provided for it or not.

CHAPTER 7: HOMOSEXUALITY & MARRIAGE

Activist Judges

It has been a steady climb for gays in relationships to be legally recognized. In 1996 the Defense of Marriage Act (DOMA) at the time protected citizens of the United States from the scourge of homosexual unions and marriages. DOMA allows the states to refuse recognition of same-sex marriages under laws of other states. The push for rights and benefits outside of marriage began in the 70s with civil unions. Hawaii was the first state to declare the constitutional prohibition against the ban on civil unions in 1993.[1]

On June 26, 2003, the United States Supreme Court by a vote of 6-3 struck down the sodomy law in Texas and by extension invalidated sodomy laws in thirteen other states, making same-sex sexual activity legal in every U.S. state and territory. In so doing the Supreme Court overturned its own ruling on the same issue in the 1986 case[2] Bowers vs. Hardwick, where it upheld a Georgia Statute and did not find a constitutional protection of sexual privacy. Now it is the law of the land for sexual deviancy and has been since 2003. This ruling fueled the gay rights movement to advance same-sex marriage in the Courts.

215

On June 26, 2013 the U.S. Supreme Court struck down the law barring federal recognition of same-sex marriage in United States vs. Windsor.³

Twenty states now, with more pending have found State amendments or statutes banning same-sex marriage unconstitutional. The President of the United States, Barack Obama became the first sitting President to declare support for legalizing same-sex marriage on May 9, 2012.⁴

Obama in his second inaugural speech said we will not reach equality "until our gay brothers and sisters are treated like anyone else under the law, for if we are truly created equal, then surely the love we commit to one another must be equal as well." God can't be too happy with this country as it is now constituted. First the Bible was removed from schools and then the Ten Commandments were removed, all by activist judges. We were kept in check by the Commandments of God, but now all restraints are off until God's holy matrimony between one man and one woman in a lifelong covenant before God is totally blasphemed. Same-sex marriage is a mockery of God's law for mankind. It is all out rebellion against the Creator. "For rebellion is as the sin of witchcraft, and

CHAPTER 7: HOMOSEXUALITY & MARRIAGE

stubbornness is as iniquity and idolatry." (1 Samuel 15:23)

It is clear that individual activist judges are helping the movement to approve same-sex marriage. In July 2014 Judge Luis Garcia has overturned the ban in his Florida county, and paved the way for the issuance of marriage licenses for same-sex couples. In California, homosexual judge Vaughn Walker overturned the ban on same-sex marriage contained in voter-approved Prop 8. In the 10th Circuit Court of Appeals, two out of three judges ordered Oklahoma to marry same-sex couples. Judges have picked up the ball on same-sex marriage since voters have turned down same-sex marriage proposals and voted for bans on the same. The pendulum is swinging wildly as the European Union's high court has refused to issue a blanket permission for same-sex marriage. On the other end of the spectrum, a judge in Australia has removed the taboo from incestuous relations. As a result of the 2003 decision against sodomy laws in Texas, we can expect the end to laws banning,

> "fornication, bigamy, adultery, adult incest, bestiality, and obscenity."[5]

Also in July of 2014, Utah and Indiana struck down laws banning same-sex marriage. It was U.S. District Judge Richard

Young in Indiana who ruled against traditional marriage. He incredibly surmised that if the gender and sexual orientation were removed, these couples would be like anyone else on anyone's block.

The 10th U.S. Circuit Court of Appeals was at it again when it ruled that Utah could no longer block gays from marriage. The number stands at twenty states that have established same-sex marriage. Some of these same judges that have single-handedly overturned same-sex marriage bans admit that they themselves are homosexual. In those cases where is the moral integrity to take themselves off the case due to conflict of interest concerns? Today, there are no judicial concerns but an agenda by activist judges determined to undermine credibility in our judicial system.

> "I have to be honest with you, when I look at each one of these cases I see an activist judge kowtowing to the homosexual lobby, ignoring precedent and overstepping the bounds of what they're supposed to do.[6]

All the laws that have been and are on the books for what seems like the entire history of the U.S. are being bypassed and ignored by judges with legal progression on their agenda. Even the laws striking down miscegenation (marriage between two people of different races), were still in favor

CHAPTER 7: HOMOSEXUALITY & MARRIAGE

of a marriage being between a man and a woman. These activist judges can rule same-sex marriage legal by judicial fiat, but that doesn't make it right. The federal level courts have taken on immense power of their own being manned by black-robed tyrants. The purposely packed courts, armed with their agenda are out to fundamentally alter the moral, cultural, faith-based, and political landscape of America. Under the guise of equal-protection in the Fourteenth Amendment, thirteen judges have changed the marriage laws in thirteen states forever.

Sin Of Homosexuality

> *"For even their women did change the natural use in to that which is against nature: And likewise also the men, leaving the natural use of the woman, burned in their lust one toward another; men with men working that which is unseemly,"* (Romans 1:26b,27)

Homosexuality is a lie from the devil and God warns that those who partake of this lifestyle will suffer judgment. The media has spread the lie that it is a mainstream idea that is accepted by most people. This has been proven false by the overwhelming rejection of same-sex marriage by the voters and the widespread rejection by the majority of the filth of homosexuality.

What the Bible tells us is that homosexuality, acts between two men and sexual acts of two women, is sin. Homosexuals, we are told in Romans 1: 24-27, because of their sin choose their sinful ways by being disobedient to God and denying that what they are doing is wrong and against God's words. God outlined His sexual boundaries for the Israelites before they entered Canaan. The Canaanites were so sinful that God was making room for His people, the Israelites, at the expense of the sinful Canaanite nations. Because of God's holiness He did this when He was reforming community life, establishing standards of holiness, and to maintain His people's identity to God. The Canaanites had broken those chains and same-gender sex was a part of Baal worship coming under judgment. Clearly, homosexuality was condemned under Moses and punished by death. Homosexual theology denies this obviously and tries to disprove the strong admonition of Paul in Romans 1:26 and 27. The homosexual theologians attempt to turn around Paul's condemnation of same-sex relations and say Paul was condemning sexual relations between heterosexuals.

Homosexuals attack Romans 1:26, 27, and especially 1 Corinthians 6:9.10, when denying God and their sin.

CHAPTER 7: HOMOSEXUALITY & MARRIAGE

> *"Be not deceived: neither fornicators, nor idolaters, nor adulterers, nor effeminate, nor abusers of themselves with mankind."* (1 Corinthians 6:9b)

Here we have three terms, fornicators, *pornos*, paramours; effeminate,*malakos,* catamites; abusers of themselves *arsenkoites,* sodomites, describing same-sex behavioral sins. The fornicators in verse 9 are paramours which are male prostitutes accepting cash payments for sex. They have no moral constraint and are corruptible for a price. The effeminate, catamites, are young boys preyed upon by homosexual pederasts who love to have anal sex with them. The abusers of themselves with mankind are the sodomites, fully grown adult men who love men.

All of these types of sinners need to repent or they will perish, which is what God's words tell us.

> *" Know ye not that the unrighteous shall not inherit the kingdom of God?"* (1 Corinthians 6:9a)

> *"But the fearful, and unbelieving, and the abominable, and murderers, and whoremongers (pornos, male prostitutes)... shall have their part in the lake which burneth with fire and brimstone: which is the second death."* (Revelation 21:8)

The Lord will severely punish all these homosexual sins along with others He has condemned. The Bible, God's book, is clear on the sin itself and the judgment and punishment.

Returning to our Scripture for this section on homosexual sin, which is Romans 1:26,27, we find virulent opposition to God's words by homosexuals. The things we find in these two verses are described by Paul as vile affections. This cannot be misinterpreted as sex between opposite genders but that sex between the same genders is not natural. Vile is a strong word used here from the Greek, *atimia*, and means without honor, dishonor, disgrace, ignominy, shameful passions, insolence. This is the complete opposite of holiness, morality, and the Godly virtues that the Lord Jesus desires of his saints to cultivate.

Regarding women, Paul states that they have left and changed the natural man and woman relationship to something that is against nature. What Paul is saying is that these women, Lesbians, have left behind their natural God-given desire for a man and resort to lusting after other women. They were doing the same thing men were doing with other men since Paul in verse 27, uses the term, "likewise also," to refer back to

CHAPTER 7: HOMOSEXUALITY & MARRIAGE

them. The men are burning in their lust for other men; likewise the women are burning in their lust for other women.

Men with men, Paul says, working that which is unseemly. The Greek word, *aschmosune*, translates the phrase "that which is unseemly." The word working means to work or do, carry out, practice these actions. Unseemly is a deformity, indecency, obscenity, nakedness, shameful parts. Strong's dictionary gives the implication of pudenda which is the neuter plural of the external genital organs of a human being, especially of a woman. This very definitely exposes the fact that the women are burning in their lust for each other's genitals. This, indeed, is the reason then that women change the natural use into that which is against nature, which is women with women. It was likewise true of the men, as with the women, that men lusted for other men, working with their genitals that which is unseemly. This is a strong indictment of the vile affections of having sex between women with women and men with men. There can be no mistake as to what the Scriptures mean. And it is a shame that these haters of God have made the message of God's repentance and redemption for sin a crime. It is a shame that they know the judgment of God will be upon them for their sin but they stubbornly continue to commit such things worthy of death.

> "For I am not ashamed of the gospel of Christ: for it is the power of God unto salvation to everyone that believeth; to the Jew first, and also to the Greek." (Romans 1:16)

A.I.D.S.

> "...and receiving in themselves that recompence of their error which was meet (due)," (Romans 1:27b)

> "Be not deceived; God is not mocked: for whatsoever a man soweth, that shall he also reap." (Galatians 6:7)

Homosexuals truly hate to be told that their actions will bring consequences. They also hate to be made aware that their same-gender lusting and working may bring about a case of AIDS. Saints are accused of being homophobes for pointing out this simple principle of sowing and reaping. It works for any working of the flesh as well as homosexuality. Christians do not hate homosexuals or have any fear of them if they are washed in the blood of Christ. The spirit of fear is of the devil. (2 Tim. 1:7) Christians also know that homosexuality is a sin against nature and is a guided attack on biblical marriage.

CHAPTER 7: HOMOSEXUALITY & MARRIAGE

The disease of AIDS is a great threat to society. It has been determined that the cause is the vile affections of men with men working unseemliness in the body. This is a horrible plague spread by promiscuous gay men. Cases of men getting very sick and dying were first observed in the 70s and 80s. At first it was called G.R.I.D. or Gay Related Immune Deficiency, but that brought an outcry to change the name. Now it is called A.I.D.S. or Acquired Immune Deficiency Syndrome.

It spread fast and hit hard in the gay community. A study in 1978 by Bell and Wineburg showed that nearly half of gay males would have over 500 sex partners during their short lifetime.[7]

The Sodomite working of sodomy is such a horrendous and evil assault to the human body's immune system, God gives it the term, abomination. This descriptive part of the immune organic system is taken from an article by a pastor in Brazil:

    The defense mechanisms are basically three:

    a. Shields surface: dermis (skin and mucosal surfaces) as a first line of defense).
    b. Protectors nonspecific (innate

immunity): macrophages, neutrophils, and NK.
c. Protectors specific (acquired immunity): lymphoid or lymphatic system. In the latter's memory and learning, with the presence of specific receptors for each molecule invasive.

Lymphocytes are of three types:

a. Type B lymphocytes: the humoral response which originate plasma cells, antibody-producing cells. Originate in the bone marrow.
b. Type T lymphocytes: destroy malignant cells and virus-infected, also helping other cells to perform their functions by secreting interleukins. These are responsible for deactivation of the immune system.
c. Lymphocyte NK (natural killer): no need to react to stimuli; are an innate immune response.

The type of T lymphocyte, also called T cells, are three subtypes:

a. Type cytotoxic or killer (TK): responsible for destroying malignant cells and virus infected. Interact with the second type of lymphocytes, helper type.
b. Type T helper (TH): responsible for

CHAPTER 7: HOMOSEXUALITY & MARRIAGE

secretion of interleukins, other cells which help to perform its functions (activation of B cells to plasma cells producing antibodies, regulation of the function of cytotoxic cells, activation of macrophages).

c. Type T suppressor (TS): responsible for disabling the immune system (initial stimulus removed, the immune response to self-antigens - autoimmune diseases).[8]

The sequence of the Acquired Immune Deficiency begins with the Sodomites introduction of semen into the bloodstream. The semen is composed of testicular secretions, seminal vesicles and prostate gland cowper, with a pH of 8.1 to 8.4. A single milliliter of semen can contain up to 120 million sperm.[9]

There are certain on-off keys that work the immune system. Certain key patterns are responsible for super-activation or the blocking of the immune system. The virus which causes the HIV response is too strong for the immune system and so far all efforts for a vaccine have failed due to this blocking of the immune system. It has also been found that a protein (IRF5) has been found in white blood cells and cannot be controlled as yet from inhibiting the immune system.

When God pronounced sodomy as an abomination he did it out of love for the human race. During the working of unseemliness, or practice of sodomizing, the attack causes damage, often irreparable to the digestive system. The result of the end walls of the intestinal tract being damaged, the inoculation of semen into the bloodstream, is a direct assault on the immune system. Semen was designed by the creator for allowing the human race to reproduce. AIDS is the body's natural response to the turning off of the immune system and the destruction of a human body from such terrible aggression. The world seeks a solution to this physical devastation by changing or circumventing the organic system that God has perfectly created. Each time man is defeated in this quest to get around God's creation, it only increases the hatred of the affected and infected community that He is constantly reaching out to. God is long-suffering and not willing of any to perish, if only the homosexual would repent of their sin God would forgive him.

> *"And the rest of the men which were not killed by these plagues yet repented not of the works of their hands,"* (Revelation 9:20a)

CHAPTER 7: HOMOSEXUALITY & MARRIAGE

Sodomite Promiscuity

Having described the intricacies of the AIDS immune syndrome, what effect is all this having on our country? On July 15, 2014, the Centers for Disease Control and Prevention a National Government study produced a measurement of American's sexual proclivities. Surprisingly they found that there are a rather small number of U.S. citizens who self-identify as homosexual bisexual, or something else. A tremendous majority identified themselves as straight. This is despite all the hype, all the propaganda put out by radical pro-homosexual groups seeking to mainstream so repugnant a behavior.

The results found that 1.6% (less than 2%) identified as being homosexual, while 0.7% considered themselves as bisexual, and 1.1% as something else. 96.6% of American adults considered themselves as straight.[10]

The second main postulate of disgust of the gay movement that will be dealt with here is the horrible reality that they're after your children! It is alarming to know that children that are abused in California and feel attracted to their same gender get counseled that they may be homosexual, lesbian, bisexual, a transgender, or anything else. They are left to their own devices if they resist that feeling for it is illegal for therapists to help turn from that back to heterosexuality."[11]

You cannot now in California, try to turn any child away from his or her darkness to the truth. How could this happen? Laws have been passed for years in California and some other states allowing more access to children by lesbian, gay, bisexual, transgender (LGBT) advocates.

In 2010 SB543 was passed which allows school staff to remove your 12+ year-old child from school without your consent, to be counseled in favor of homosexuality by LGBT counselors, under the guise of "mental health counseling." ACR82(2010 makes schools into "discrimination-free zones" that will "counsel" anyone who speaks or writes against LCBT behavior.

SB572 (2009) forces celebration of "Harvey Milk Day" yearly, about May 22nd, teaching children to admire a homosexual predator, who sexually abused males as young as 16.

SB777 (2007) requires teaching all children from kindergarten upward that gender is determined at birth, and can be

CHAPTER 7: HOMOSEXUALITY & MARRIAGE

chosen later, based on feelings.[12]

In California they teach from kindergarten through college, by indoctrination, that various forms of sexual perversion are good, healthy expressions of "who they are."[13]

Anyone who warns children that the opposite is true is labeled as bad. This includes pastors, preachers, medical staff who warn children of the dangers of these lifestyles are branded as enemies of the state. If you know the truth and wish to enlighten children with it, not poisoning them with filth and disease, that makes one the enemy. That kind of behavior, not deviant sexual behavior, will be reported to the proper authorities.

Why would LGBT people want to go after the children? First of all they cannot reproduce. Men with men, women with women cannot reproduce. They must recruit uneducated, unreached children into their perverted lifestyle. They are helping to write and see laws passed that make it very easy for children to be brought into their ranks. The LBGT people are unashamed to present their lifestyle to kids. It is legal for them to impose themselves on children, because no one is going to stop them from the law's perspective. Armed with the gospel of Jesus

Christ, all believer parents, and all parents in general, must love their own children with the truth. It must start very, very young; as young as possible. Children must be inoculated with the truth, against he lies of the devil.

Unlawful Marriages

In Leviticus 18:6-18, God details what is forbidden as in regards to marrying relations and others He forbids. This is in response to the Israelites, who have left Egypt and are in the wilderness, not to do as the Egyptians who were guilty of every one of these sinful relations.

> *"After the doings of the Land of Egypt, wherein ye dwelt, shall ye not do:"*
> (Leviticus 18:3a)

He was the Lord their God and He wanted them to obey Him so that things would go well with them. Egypt had just been judged with devastating plagues, and their army had been destroyed in the Red Sea, something that they have never fully recovered from till this day. The Lord was leading the Israelites to Canaan where the Canaanites were going to be facing judgment for the same types of sins as were left behind in Egypt.

CHAPTER 7: HOMOSEXUALITY & MARRIAGE

> *"And after the doings of the Land of Canaan, whether I bring you, shall ye not do: neither shall ye walk in their ordinances."* (Leviticus 18:3b)

It is true that there were homosexual and same-sex unions in Egypt as well as Canaan as it will be shown. The listing in this chapter of Leviticus of these forbidden relations was intended to forbid the marrying of any of these relations. Unfortunately, the law has been changed here in the U.S. to allow same-sex marriage, as it was in Canaan and Egypt. Soon, it is projected that the rest of these types of relationships and marriages will be lawful in America when God expressly says that they are unlawful. These were big reasons for the judgments on Egypt and Canaan, as they will be for America. These were written for a warning of judgment then, and are listed now as a warning of impending judgment now. The Gentile people did not listen then and it would be presumptuous to think they will listen now.

It must be restated that marriage is a divine institution. It was created by God and given to mankind for their comfort, and it is honorable for the propagation of the human race. These marriage laws given by God were in support of honorable marriages and as a boundary against the corrupt nature of man. Marriage between a man and a woman to enact them becoming one flesh, was to unite those who before were not united. These then, on the list were not to be united to become one flesh by being joined in the divine institution. These relations between families are unequal as far as marriage goes, and founded in blood or by marriage, and are perpetual and causes great confusion if those boundaries are removed and made equal by marriage.

Such marriages as brothers with sisters cannot be nowadays, for generation by generation they would be a world to itself where we are members one of another. Marriage put to rest incestuous combinations so as to not profane God. Another reason for these being forbidden marriages would be to keep uncleanness out of marriage and all lascivious behavior that has the appearance of evil. These inter-family relations must be free to love one another, in a Godly and pure way. These were shown to reasonable men to make plain that a man is forbidden from marrying any of those with whom he had married into.

> *"None of you shall approach to any that is near of kin to him, to uncover their nakedness: I am the Lord."* (Leviticus 18:6)

CHAPTER 7: HOMOSEXUALITY & MARRIAGE

These are the prohibitions God was giving for the rest of time.

It should be understood that those in the early days of humanity on earth that very near of kin must have had to be married. Brothers and sisters would have married each other such as in the family of Adam. Necessity formed the boundaries then but no longer exist as such today. Two reasons why are:

1. That the duties owing by nature to relatives might not be confounded with those of a social or political kind; for could a man be a brother and a husband, a son and a husband, at the same time, and fulfill the duties of both? Impossible.
2. That by intermarrying with other families, the bonds of social compact might be strengthened and extended, so that the love of our neighbor, etc., might at once be felt to be not only a maxim of sound policy, but also a very practicable and easy duty; and thus feuds, divisions, and wars be prevented.[14]

The coming conquering and extermination of the ancient Canaanites that the Israelites were to execute through God's power was a result of the abominations they

MARRIAGE, DIVORCE, & REMARRIAGE

had practiced in polluting the land. These verses in Leviticus (7-18) point to some of these and warn others, like the United States of America, that if you pollute the land likewise, God will judge.

The prohibited relations and forbidden marriages:

Verse 7: Between mother and son.

Verse 8: Between stepmother and son, your father's wife.

Verse 9: One cannot marry your sister or half-sister by mother.

Verse 10: You cannot marry your granddaughter.

Verse 11: Do not marry the daughter or half-daughter of the father.

Verse 12: No marriage between nephew and father's sister, (aunt).

Verse 13: You cannot marry your mother's sister (aunt).

Verse 14: No marriage between a man and a wife of father's brother.

Verse 15: Prohibition of man marrying his daughter-in-law.

CHAPTER 7: HOMOSEXUALITY & MARRIAGE

Verse 16: No marriage of a man and his brother's wife (sister-in-law).

Verse 17: You cannot marry a girl and her mother. Between a father and step-daughter; a father and step-granddaughter; and a husband and his mother-in-law.

Verse 18: Prohibition of a husband marrying his sister-in-law.

The penalties for a man marrying close relatives that violated God's principles for family values which are highly valued, are severe.

We come to Leviticus 18:22 to prove to those who do not believe that God has prohibited and judges homosexuality and same-sex marriage. It is here in the Bible. God condemns it in the Old Testament as well as in the New Testament.

Verse 18: *"Thou shalt not lie with mankind, as with womankind. It is abomination."*

The Hebrew word for abomination is, *Toebah*, and identifies anything as being very offensive to God. It means to God it is detestable, impure, wicked, profane, polluted and to be abhorred. God is making it clear that homosexual acts between people of the same gender are abhorrent and there is to be absolutely no marriage between the same. God punished all evil-doers before and he will again today.

> "Defile not yourselves in any of these things: for in all these the nations are defiled which I cast out before you: and the land is defiled: therefore, I do visit the iniquity thereof upon it, and the land itself vomiteth out her inhabitants." (Leviticus 18:24-25)

It should be obvious to Christians that these are serious crimes and they should not be indulged in. In strong language God identifies the sin, convicts those who are committing the abomination, and removes the perpetrators.

Jesus And Same-Sex Marriage

As it has already been shown, our Lord Jesus Christ has said definite truths about homosexuality and same-sex marriage. Ignorance of the Holy Scriptures will prove eternally costly and is very dangerous to those who thumb their nose at God. He created man and woman, instituted holy marriage as being between a man and a woman, and set out severe penalties for those who advocate same-sex marriage. Homosexuality is against God's created order and only corrupts what God says. God tells

CHAPTER 7: HOMOSEXUALITY & MARRIAGE

us in Romans 1 that homosexuality is called "vile affections." (V 26), "against nature" (V 26), "unseemly" (V 27), "error" (V 27), and of a "reprobate mind" (V 28).[15]

If it is looked at closely, the proposition of same-sex marriage is ludicrous. Homosexuality as a movement in the U.S. is founded on promiscuity. It has already been mentioned earlier of the hundreds of sexual partners a homosexual male has in his life. Even before the tidal wave of same-sex marriage hit, the average length of a gay relationship lasted only 18 months.

Another fact is that in states that have same-sex marriage, few men marry. Between the years 2004 and 2008, only 37% of same-sex marriages in Massachusetts involved men.[16]

The gay movement is actually a mess. With below 2% of the population, men that have sex with other men account for more than half of new HIV infections. Homosexual men are 44-88% more likely to be infected with HIV than other men. African-American men had even higher rates than white men. These are all Centers For Disease Control statistics. It boils down to that 50% of homosexual men are believed to be HIV positive, since 44% are unaware they are even infected.

The impact of the spreading of HIV and other serious diseases by the homosexual revolution is devastating. 2-4% of the population is bisexual and they make up the majority of the LGBT movement. This is the avenue of transmission of these diseases to the heterosexual population, with 70% of HIV infections in women being a result of this contact.

As of now there is no proof that same-sex marriage has had any noticeable decrease of gay promiscuity. The interest in marriage is not the most important point to this movement. The impact of the marriages that are same-sex and the continuance of outside relationships not held in by any boundaries, is a total mockery to and a destruction of God's divine institution of marriage.

Traditional Marriage Of a Man And a Woman

Then there is the reality of lesbian marriage being very advantageous for women. The two lesbians will be in a close relationship with government. Their children will be conceived from serial extramarital meetings. The men will believe that no children will result from the encounter. Then it works out that the two women keep their

CHAPTER 7: HOMOSEXUALITY & MARRIAGE

incomes, and they depend on the government to force however many men to provide many tax-free "child support" incomes.

Another political-social phenomenon is happening. The gays wish to take over the Conservative movement. Gay intrusion into its ranks is alienating voters. Lawsuits at the Supreme Court level will force more homosexuality on America. More conservatives are being bullied into supporting gay marriage. The demise of heterosexual marriage is destroying the country. Multicultural marriage is dividing America. Heterosexual marriage needs to be restored to earlier levels and be considered the social norm. Gay marriage in this country, being Anti-God at its core, should never have been given a chance to succeed.

We can stipulate that the subject of same-sex marriage is not found per-se in the Bible. The subject of traditional marriage is there, but it does not mean that same-sex marriage is not prohibited by God. All the evidence points to the position that God is not for it, as it is included in the list of forbidden marriages of Leviticus 18. Both the Old and the New Testaments speak clearly about homosexuality and God's condemnation and judgment of that abomination.

The story of the two angels visiting Lot in Sodom in Genesis 19:1-14 illustrates the point.

> *"The men of the city, the men of Sodom, surrounded the house, both young and old...Bring them out to us that we may have relations with them."* (Genesis 19:4,5b).

This is clear that the men of Sodom wanted to have sex with the angels of God who were in the form of men. The angels were there to warn Lot and bring him and his family to safety before the place was destroyed by God just after sunrise the next day. It was not a case of inhospitality as the false homosexual theologians teach in error. It was judgment. In 2 Peter 2:6-10 God reveals that the homosexual should take notice and learn a wise lesson: "And turning the cities of Sodom and Gomorrah into ashes condemned them with an overthrow, making them an ensample unto those that after should live ungodly;" (2 Peter 2:6). To have unnatural sexual desires like those in Abraham's times led to destruction. This is the lesson that those who engage in sex with their own gender are under the judgment of God the same today as they were then. That was the example to those alive today.

CHAPTER 7: HOMOSEXUALITY & MARRIAGE

> *"Even as Sodom and Gomorrah and the cities about them in like manner, giving themselves over to fornication, and going after strange flesh, are set forth for an example, suffering the vengeance of eternal fire."* (Jude 7)

God detests the homosexual lifestyle and behavior.

> *"If a man also lie with mankind, as he lieth with a woman, both of them have committed an abomination:"* (Leviticus 20:13)

In the New Testament God condemns the behavior of going after strange flesh as already discussed in Romans 1:26,27. Scripture says that homosexuals will not see the Kingdom of God. In 1 Corinthians 6:9-10:

> *"Know ye not that the unrighteous shall not inherit the Kingdom of God? Be not deceived: neither fornicators, nor idolaters, nor adulterers, nor effeminate, nor abusers of themselves with mankind."* (homosexuals).

The admonition is repeated again in 1 Timothy 1:9-10. Homosexuality is clearly addressed in the Bible. God is direct, clear, and uncompromising, telling homosexuals as well as all sinners that the blood of Jesus Christ would cover all their sins if only they would repent.

It has been covered about how God feels about marriage between a man and a woman. That is how he created man and woman for the institution of marriage.

> *"So God created man in his own image, in the image of God created he him; male and female created he them."* (Genesis 1:27)

> *"And Adam called his wife's name Eve;"* (Genesis 3:20a)

Christ affirms the relationship as one of a man and a woman married in the eyes of God.

> *"But from the beginning of the creation God made them male and female."* (Mark 10:6)

Marriage is not to be taken lightly or made a mockery of. It is special and blessed of God and honored within society.

> *"Marriage is honorable in all, and the bed undefiled: but whoremongers and adulterers God will judge."* (Hebrews 13:4)

These are the statements of God on homosexuality and his statements on marriage.

CHAPTER 7: HOMOSEXUALITY & MARRIAGE

What can we deduce as God's feelings on same-sex marriage? Putting the two opposing camps together a number of reasons God opposes same-sex marriage would be:

1. The lifestyle violates all the Godly principles of a holy and harmonious union as God intended.
2. Unnatural and corrupt desires constitute same-sex marriage and are opposed by God.
3. Same-sex marriage openly thumbs its nose at God and satisfies a carnal will which is enmity with God.
4. Abominations, such as same-sex behaviors bring God's wrath instead of His blessings.
5. Same-sex marriages are not God's ideal that He created from the beginning.
6. Children are not naturally conceived in a same-sex marital environment, thereby is against God's command to multiply for the survival of the human race.
7. There is no praise or honor to God in same-sex marriages as there is in hetero-traditional marriages.

Based on God's revelations to man through His words, it would be impossible for an all-knowing, all-powerful, holy God to endorse something such as same-sex, homosexual marriage. This is an abomination in God's eyes and it will bring judgment upon this country and all others who believe the same, according to the words of God.

END NOTES

Introduction

1. Juan Enriquez. *A New You*. Foreign Policy Magazine. May-June 2009.
2. Michael Snyder. *The Economics of Marriage.* May, 2014.
3. Ibid.
4. Ibid.
5. Ibid.
6. Ibid.
7. Ibid.

Chapter 1

1. *Marriage Laws in the United States.* World Christianship Ministries. Fresno, CA.
2. *The Constitution and Our Religious Freedom.* World Christianship Ministries. Fresno, CA.
3. *Historical Evolution of Christian Marriage.* www.wikigender.org
4. Ibid.
5. *Consent in History, Theory and Practice.* www.autonomy.essex.ac.uk

6. Ibid.
7. *From Fleet Street to Gretna Green.* www.jenpayne10.info/clandestine
8. Ibid.
9. *Consanguinity.* www.en.wikipedia.org/coanguinity
10. *Consummation.* www.en.wikipedia.org/consummation
11. *Historical Evolution with Christian Marriage.*
12. *Miscegnenation.* Webster online. www.merriam-webster.com
13. *Misegnenation.* www.en.metapedia.org
14. Ibid.

Chapter 2

1. McGee. *Song of Solomon.* Thru the Bible, Pasadena, CA. 1977. P97.
2. Morris. *Wisdom of Solomon.* P32.

Chapter 3

1. David Cloud. *Encyclopedia of the Bible;Judgment.* PP 256-257.
2. Panton. *Judgment Seat of Christ.* P. 22.

ENDNOTES

Chapter 4

1. *Fornication.* Christiananswers.net. Web Bible Encyclopedia.
2. D.A. Waite. *The Third 200 Questions Answered.* PP. 79,80.
3. Dr. Bruce Malina. *Does Porneia Mean Fornication?* P17.
4. Ibid. Footnote P17.
5. *Bet Hillel and Bet Shammai.* JewishEncyclopedia.com.
6. *Shammai.* JewishEncyclopedia.com.
7. Babylonian Talmud (Talmud Bavli), Tractate Giffan, 90a.
8. *Divorce.* JewishEncyclopedia.com.
9. Ibid.
10. Ibid.
11. *Get.* (*Bill of Divorce*) JewishEncyclopedia.com.
12. D.A. Waite. *Third 200 Questions Answered.* P95.
13. D.A. Waite. *The First 200 Questions Answered.* P129.
14. *Betrothal.* Wikipedia.org.
15. Ibid.
16. *The Betrothal.* www.chabad.org

17. David W. Jones. *The Betrothal View.* PP 68-85.
18. Ibid. P69.

Chapter 5

1. John Mayone. *Southern Divorce.* 2004. P18.
2. Wick Allison. *D. Magazine.* City Magazine of Dallas, Texas.
3. Dr. Kirk DiVietro. *Cleaning-up Hazardous Materials.* P15.
4. Dr. D.A. Waite. *A Warning!!* Preface. p vii.
5. Ibid. p viii.
6. Ibid. p viii.
7. Ibid. p viii.
8. Ibid. p viii.
9. Spurgeon. *The Blind Eye and the Deaf Ear.* 1877.
10. Birth Certificate of Gail Anne Ludwig. Office of Vital Statistics. Columbus, Ohio.
11. Gail Anne Latessa vs. Terry Latessa. Case #74-DR-1543. February 10, 1975.
12. Ibid.

13. Gail Anne Kaleda vs. Frank A. Kaleda. Case #84-CV0652, August 6, 1984.

14. Ibid.

15. Taped during two-hour lecture at Berean Baptist Church. May 19, 1996.

16. Taped at Temple Baptist Church, Tennessee. 1996.

17. *Riplinger's Testimony* Interview with Mrs. Yvonne Waite.

18. Ibid.

19. Ibid.

20. Ibid.

21. Dr. D.A Waite. *The Fourth 200 Questions Answered.* P88.

22. Ibid. P89.

23. Dr. D.A. Waite. *Gail Riplinger's KJB and Multiple Inspiration Heresy.* P5.

24. Ibid. pp 6-7.

25. Peter Ruckman. *The Alexandrian Cult.* Part I. P6.

26. Peter Ruckman. *The Full Cup.* P225.

27. Ibid. P273.

28. Ibid. P276.
29. Dr. D.A. Waite. *First Timothy*. 2007. pp 87-88.

CHAPTER 6

1. Crouzel. *L 'eglise Primitive*. p54.
2. Heth and Wenham. *Jesus and Divorce*. p35.
3. Bettenson. Editor. *The Early Christian Fathers*. p132.
4. Ibid. p150.
5. Heth and Wenham. *Jesus and Divorce*. p37.
6. Ibid. p74.
7. Ibid. p76.
8. Ibid. p86.
9. Dr. David Brown. *Marriage, Divorce and Remarriage*. p4.
10. David W. Jones. *The Betrothal View*. p69.
11. Heth and Wenham. *Jesus and Divorce*. p175.
12. Dr. David Brown. *Marriage, Divorce and Remarriage*. P5.
13. W. Fisher-Hunter. *The Divorce Problem*. P95.

14. Ibid. p96.
15. Ibid. p96.
16. Ibid. p97.

CHAPTER 7

1. *Same-Sex Marriage*. Wikipedia.org.
2. Ibid.
3. Ibid.
4. Ibid.
5. Antonin Scalia. *Dissent to Lawrence vs Texas*.
6. Daniel Schmid. *Liberty Counsel*.
7. *Homosexuality: A Study of Diversion*. Simon & Schuster. 1978. p308.
8. *Homosexuality*. A Pastor in Brazil. Feb. 2012.
9. Ibid.
10. CDC Study. *How Many Americans Are Homosexual?* www.tpnn.com.
11. Battle Cry. July/August 2014.
12. Ibid.
13. Ibid.
14. Adam Clarke. *Commentary Vol*

1. p570.
15. David Cloud. *Jesus and Same-Sex Marriage*. July 2013.
16. David Usher and Cynthia Davis. *Homosexual Promiscuity*. Newwithviews.com. Sept. 2012.

BIBLIOGRAPHY

BOOKS

Adams, Jay E. *Christian Living in the Home*. Presbyterian and Reformed Publishers. Phillipsburg, New Jersey. 1972.

_____ *Marriage, Divorce, and Remarriage in the Bible*. Zondervan Publishers. Grand Rapids, Michigan. 1980.

Ballew, Dr. Stinnett D. *The Home: America's Number One Problem*. Church Outreach Missions and Evangelism. Resaca, Georgia. 1997.

Baker, Karl M. *The Marriage and Divorce Controversy.* Calvary Baptist Church. Beaufort, South Carolina.

Bullock, Hassell C. *The Old Testament Poetic Books.* Moody Press, Chicago. 1979. pp 223-254.

Criswell, W.A. *The Doctrine of the Church.* Convention Press. Nashville, Tennessee. 1980.

Davis, Bryan. *Spit and Polish for Husbands*. AMG Publishers. Chattanooga, Tennessee. 2004.

DiVietro, Dr. Kirk. *Cleaning up Hazardous Waste.* Dean Burgon Society Press. Collingswood, NJ. 2010.

Dobson, Edward G. *What the Bible Really Says About Marriage, Divorce, and Remarriage.* Fleming H. Revell Company. New Jersey. 1986.

Ehrlich, Eugene. *The Highly Selective Dictionary for the Extraordinarily Literate.* Harbor Collins Publishers. 1997.

Fisher-Hunter, William. *The Divorce Problem.* MacNeish Publishers. Waynesboro, PA 1952.

Greene, Oliver B. Edited by Mrs. Greene. *Marriage, Divorce, and Remarriage.* The Gospel Hour, Inc. Greensville, South Carolina.

Hawkins, Rev. Gilbert. *Marriage Lasts a Lifetime.* Brethren Missionary Herald Co. Winena Lake, Indiana 1975.

Henry, Matthew. *Matthew Henry's Commentary. Volume III. Job to Song of Solomon.* MacDonald Publishing. pp 1052-1101.

Heth, William A. and Wenham, Gordon J. *Jesus and Divorce.* Thomas Nelson Publishers. 1985.

BIBLIOGRAPHY

Hopewell, Wm. J. Jr. *Marriage and Divorce.* Niles and Phipps Lithographers, Inc. Bingingham, NY. 1976.

House, Wayne H. (Editor). *Divorce and Remarriage.* Four Christian Views. Intervaristy Press. Downers Grove, Illinois. 1990.

Ironside, H.A. *Addresses on the Song of Solomon.* Loizeaux Brothers, Inc. 1933. (copied from internet.) Chapters 1-7.

Laney, Carl J. *The Divorce Myth.* Bethany House Publishers. Minneapolis, Minnesota. 1981.

MacArthur, John. *On Divorce: Matthew 19:1-12.* Moody Press. Chicago. 1985.

Mayoue, John C. *Southern Divorce.* PSG Books. Dallas, Texas. 2004. pp 7-43.

McGee, Vernon J. *Ecclesiastes and Song of Solomon.* Thru the Bible. Pasadena, CA. 1988. pp 97-187.

_____ *Marriage and Divorce.* Thomas Nelson Publishers. Nashville, Tennessee. 1988.

Morris, Henry M. *The Wisdom of Solomon.* Master Books, Inc. Green Forest,

AR. 2001. pp 13-61.

O'Brien, Aletheia. *Who is Gail Riplinger? A Warning for God's Sheep*.

Panton, D.M. *The Judgment Seat of Christ*. Schoettle Publishing. Hayesville, NC. 1984.

Rice, John R. *Divorce, the Wreck of Marriage*. Sword of the Lord Publishers. Murfreesboro, TN. 1946.

Ruckman, Dr. Peter S.. *Marriage, Divorce, and Remarriage*. Bible Baptist Bookstore. Pensacola, FL. 1980.

Shaff, Tom. *1 Corinthians*. Family Station's Inc. Oakland, California. 1987.

Sorenson, David. *Have a Heavenly Marriage*. Sword of the Lord Publishers. Murfreesboro, TN. 2000.

Tabb, Dr. M.H. *God and Divorce*. Foundation Ministries. Fort Walton, Beach, FL. 1983.

Waite, Dr. D.A. Waite. *A Warning!! on Gail Riplinger* Bible for Today Press. Collingswood, NJ. 2010.

_____ *First Peter*. BFT Press. Collingswood, NJ. 2001. Pp 127-129.

BIBLIOGRAPHY

_____ *Making Marriage Melodious.* Bible for Today Press. Collingswood, NJ. 2003.

_____ *The First 200 Questions Answered.* BFT Press. Collingswood, NJ. pp 129, 149.

_____ *The Second 200 Questions Answered.* BFT Press. Collingswood, NJ. pp 129, 130-140.

_____ *The Fifth 200 Questions Answered* BFT Press. Collingswood, NJ. pp 88-91; 102-105.

_____ *Revelation.* Bible for Today Press. Collingswood, NJ. 2012. pp 463-473; 843-860.

_____ *The Third 200 Questions Answered.* BFT Press. Collingswood, NJ. 2011.

pp 79-80; 94-95; 163.

_____ *Fundamentalist Distortions On Bible Versions.* BFT Press. Collingswood, NJ 1999.

_____ *Bob Jones University's Errors On Bible Preservation.*

BFT Press. Collingswood, NJ. 2006.

_____ *The Superior Foundation of The King James Bible*. BFT Press. Collingswood, NJ. 2008.

_____ *Brief Analysis of the N.I.V. Inclusive Language Edition*. BFT #2768. Collingswood, NJ. 1997.

_____ *A Critical Answer To James Price*. BFT Press. Collingswood, NJ. 2009.

Williams, Dr. H.D. T*he Miracle of Biblical Inspiration*. The Old Path Publications, Inc. Cleveland, GA. 2009.

_____ *Word for Word Translating of the Received Texts*. BFT Press. Collingswood, NJ. 2007.

Wilmington, H.L. *The Complete Book of Bible Lists*. Tyndale Publishers. Wheaton, IL. 1987.

ARTICLES

Adultery, Fornication. Bible Scriptures bySubjects. www.Apostolic_Churches.net/bible/sbs/adultery and fornication. 23 pages.

BIBLIOGRAPHY

Brown, Dr. David L. *Marriage, Divorce and Remarriage.* www.logosresourcepages.org/counseling/divorce.htm.

Brug, John F., *Forward in Christ.* Nov. 1996. www.wels.net.

Burke, Matthew. *How Many Americans are Homosexual?* CDC Study. July, 2014.

Burns, Dr. Cathy. *Divorce and Remarriage.* Sharing. Mt. Carmel, PA.

_____ *What is Miscegenation?* Mt. Carmel, PA.

Clarke, Adam. *Commentary. Volume 1* Abington-Cokesbury Press. pp 570-571.

Cloud, David. *Gail Riplinger's Lies to Dr. and Mrs. D.A. Waite.* www.wayoflife.org. Nov, 2009.

_____ *Jesus and Same-Sex Marriage.* July, 2013.

_____ *Obama and Homosexual Love.* Wayoflife.org. Jan, 2012.

_____ *The Church Fathers: A Door to Rome.* www.wayoflife.org pp1-2.

_____ *Way of Life Encyclopedia.* Bethel Baptist Print Ministry. London, Ontario. 2nd Edition. 1997. pp 288-289.

_____ *What about Peter Ruckman?* O Timothy Magazine. Volume II, Issue 11. 1994.

Conner, David. *Jesus Teaches on Divorce.* Life in Christ Study.

Crowder, Providence. *Marriage: A Social Contract or Holy Matrimony?* www.minorityrepublican.com. Feb, 2012. pp 1-2.

Curtis, Donald E. *"Boundaries of Godly Sexuality."* www.Bible.org.

Dave, Dr. *Ruckman's Personal Controversy and Views on Divorced Pastors.* Ruckmanism.com. 2010.

Daniels, David W. *They're After Your Children.* Battle Cry. July/Aug 2004. Chick Publications. Ontario, CA.

EarlyChristianHistory.info. *Heresies:Montanism.* pp 1-3.

Enriquez, Juan. *A New You Foreign Policy* #172. www.questia.com. pp 1-5.

BIBLIOGRAPHY

Gotquestions.org. *What Is Montanism?"* pp 1-2.

Grab, John Edward Jr. *Divorce and Remarriage.* A Thesis submitted to Liberty University. Fall 2011.

Hayward, John. *Mozilla Thought Crime, IRS Corruption, and the Devaluation of Marriage.* Breitbart. 2014. pp 1-3.

Headheartland.org. *The Happiness of the Christian Family.* 2014. pp 1-2.

Henry, Clinton D. Perspective Paper on Marriage, Divorce, and Remarriage. *God's Declaration on Practices.* pp 7-10.

Henry, Jerry. *Marriage, Divorce, Adultery, and Remarriage.* Bible For Today #2254.

Hohmann, Leo. *13 Judges Responsible for Same-Sex Marriage in 13 States.* www.wnd.com. June 2014. pp 1-3.

Ironside, H.A. *Addresses on the Song of Solomon.* Loizeau Brothers, Inc. 1933. www.Baptistbiblebelievers.com.

Jerome, Rev. Norman B. *Marriage, Divorce, and Remarriage.* Tract #B-303. Tabernacle Baptist Church.

Jones, David W. *The Betrothal View of Divorce and Remarriage.* Bibliotheca Sacra. 165. (Jan – Mar 2008). pp 68-85.

Keller, J. D. *Apostasy and Divorce.* Independent Bible Church Movement. Northern Maine. 1977.

Keifer, James. *Justin Martyr, Philosopher, Apologist, and Martyr.* Biographicalsketchers.org. pp 1-4.

Kostenberger, Andreas J. *The Bible's Teaching on Marriage and the Family.* Family Research Council pp 1-6.

Lackey, Bruce. *Divorce and Remarriage.* Way of Life Encyclopedia. Bethel Baptist Print Ministry. London, Ontario, 2nd Edition 1977 pp 119-122.

Lawrence vs. Texas. En.wikipedia.org. pp 1-2.

Lively, Scott. *Sexuality and Gender Identity.* Model Bylaw Amendment For Churches. Scottlively.com.

Malina, Dr. Bruce. *Does Porneia Mean Fornication?* Novum Testamentum. 1972. pp 1-8.

McFall, Leslie. *Critique of the Betrothal Solution.* Unpublished Articles on Divorce.

BIBLIOGRAPHY

IMF12.wordpress.com.

Novak, M. *Divorce and Remarriage Cults. The Betrothal View. How the Divorce-to-Repent Explain 1 Corinthians 7.* 2012. www.divorceandremarriage cults.com.

Pastor in Brazil. *Homosexuality – An Organic Response to an Abominable Behavior?* Feb 2012. pp 1-4.

PCM Academy. *What Does God Say About Same-Sex Marriage?* Pleaseconvinceme.com. 2012.

Pruch, James M. *Marriage, Divorce, and Remarriage: An Evangelical Position Paper.* Liberty Theological Seminary. July 2012.

Rhodes, Melvin. *Same-Sex Marriage.* www.ucg.org. pp 1-7.

Same-Sex Marriage in the United States. En.wikipedia.org. pp 1-2.

Smith, David L. *Divorce and Remarriage From the Early Church to John Wesley.* www.theologicalstudies.org. pp 1-14.

Smith, Ray L. *Is Homosexuality A Sin?* Bible_Truths.com pp 3-11.

Spence, Dr. H.T. *The Powers of Fornication.* Straightway. Christian Purities Fellowship. June/July 2003. pp 1-5.

Spiess, Tim. *Marriage, Divorce, and Remarriage.* www.jesusfamilies.org. pp 1-25.

Supreme Court of Alabama. *Jaine M. Ruckman vs. Peter S. Ruckman.* Dec. 1962. Findacase.com.

The Biblical Evangelist. *The Sad Case of Peter Ruckman* B.F.T. #1708. 1989.

Unger's Bible Dictionary. *Marriage.* Moody Press. Chicago 1973. pp 697-702.

Unruh, Bob. *Activist Judges Push 'Gay Marriage'.* www.wnd.com. July, 2014 pp 1-4.

Usher and Davis. *Homosexual Promiscuity.* Newswithviews.com. Sept, 2012.

Wikipedia. *Engagement.* www.en.wikipedia.org/wiki/engagement.

INDEX OF WORDS AND PHRASES

Abraham, 25, 30, 44, 55, 128, 129, 203, 242
Adultery, 118, 120, 162, 200, 260, 263
AIDS, 224, 225, 228, 229
Amana, 73
Anglican Church, 35
Apostasy, 45, 264
Arizona, 28
Aryans, 42
Association of American Psychiatrists, 214
Baal, 91, 220
Babylon, 26, 127
Barack Hussein Obama, 12
Bashemath, 25
Bathsheba, 60, 71, 73
Bell and Wineburg, 225
Bema, 103, 104
Betrothal, 131, 132, 133, 200, 202, 249, 250, 252, 264, 265
Bible Believers' Bulletin, 166
Bishop, 182
Boalhamon, 100
Book of Common Prayer, 35
Bridegroom, 53, 85, 101
California, 29, 217, 229, 230, 231, 258, 273
Canaanite, 220
Canticle, 57
Catholic Church, 37, 186
Centers for Disease Control, 18, 229
Chuppah, 30
Church, 13, 14, 15, 21, 33, 36, 43, 44, 45, 50, 51, 52, 53, 54, 57, 58, 63, 65, 66, 68, 72, 73, 74,

78, 84, 85, 86, 87, 88, 91, 92, 93, 94, 95, 96, 97, 98, 99, 100, 101, 110, 132, 133, 135, 136, 139, 142, 144, 145, 149, 150, 151, 156, 166, 167, 168, 169, 170, 177, 182, 183, 184, 185, 186, 187, 193, 194, 197, 199, 205, 207, 211, 251, 255, 261, 263, 264, 265, 273

Civil War, 140
Clandestine, 34, 35, 36
Cohabitation, 31, 33, 34
Consanguinity, 36, 37, 248
Consent, 31, 34, 247
Conservative movement, 241
Consummation, 31, 37, 39, 248
Council of Trent, 186
Crouzel, 182, 252
Crowns, 111, 112
David Cloud, 109, 161, 162, 248, 254
David W. Jones, 132, 250, 252
Defense of Marriage Act, 215
Divorce, 15, 42, 127, 132, 139, 140, 165, 166, 171, 175, 194, 195, 196, 200, 205, 206, 210, 249, 250, 252, 255, 256, 257, 258, 261, 262, 263, 264, 265, 266
Dr. Henry M. Morris, 117
Dr. James Sightler, 155
Dr. McGee, 58
Economics, 16, 247
Egypt, 64, 232, 233
Elijah, 91
Engineers, 9

Erasmus, 184, 186, 187, 188, 189, 190, 191, 194, 198, 199
Essene, 127
Exception clause, 198
Family, 9, 139, 258, 263, 264
Fascist, 12
Felix, 106
Fleet Street, 35, 36, 248
Fornication, 117, 120, 123, 249, 260, 264, 266
Franklin Kaleda, 150
Gail Riplinger, 142, 147, 148, 151, 152, 155, 157, 159, 160, 161, 162, 163, 251, 258, 261
Gallio, 106
Get, 249
Gold, 2, 56, 109
Good Shepherd, 63
Gratian, 40
Greek, 16, 57, 106, 111, 115, 117, 118, 120, 143, 147, 154, 158, 159, 164, 170, 179, 186, 199, 204, 222, 223, 224
Ham, 43
Harlot, 21
Hebrew, 11, 16, 48, 65, 88, 106, 110, 129, 143, 147, 158, 159, 164, 237
Hephzibah, 50
Heresies, 262
Heresy, 142, 163, 251
Hermas, 177, 178, 180
Hesbon, 90
Hillel, 15, 125, 126, 127, 128, 183, 249
HIV, 227, 239, 240
Holy Spirit, 66, 70, 77, 98, 99, 100, 181
Homosexuality, 219, 238, 239, 243, 253, 265
Illinois, 29, 257
Incestuous, 36
Indian Nation, 29

Inspiration, 142, 163, 251, 260
Israelites, 32, 44, 206, 220, 232, 235
Jacobean, 147
Jehovah, 23, 32, 49, 58
Jews, 15, 25, 42, 43, 58, 106, 116, 127, 131, 176, 177, 192, 198, 199, 200
John Owen, 123
Josephus, 128
Judith, 25
Justin Martyr, 179, 180, 264
Karl Baker, 166, 168
Kent State, 149, 150
Ketubbah, 30
Kiddushin, 132
King David, 60, 71, 119
King Josiah, 50
Leah, 25
Lebanon, 74, 83, 91
Lesbians, 222
LGBT, 214, 230, 231, 240
Lincoln, 41
Lord Chancellor Hardwicke, 36
Lymphocytes, 226
Maimonides, 129
Metaphorically, 118
Michael Riplinger, 149, 150, 151, 152, 153, 159, 160
Middle Ages, 32
Miscegenation, 40, 41, 43, 261
Mischling, 42
Mischnaic, 128
Montanist, 180, 181
Mosaic Covenant, 32
Mount Hermon, 73
Mrs. Yvonne Waite, 151, 158, 159, 251
Myrrh, 64
Naamah, 62, 63, 64, 65, 66, 68, 70, 71, 72, 74, 76, 77, 79, 80, 81, 83, 84, 86, 87, 88, 89, 90,

91, 92, 93, 94, 95, 96, 97, 98, 99, 100, 101
Nazis, 42
New Evangelical Movement, 137
Papal, 32
Pastor D.A. Waite, 142, 147, 158, 273
Permissive, 32
Peter Ruckman, 103, 142, 165, 166, 167, 169, 171, 251, 262, 266
Pharisees, 15, 169, 184, 203
Philadelphia, 100
Philo, 128
Pilate, 106
Polygamy, 25, 177
Pomegranate, 96
Porneia, 118, 123, 132, 249, 264
Promiscuity, 229, 254, 266
Rachel, 25
Rapture, 51
Rehoboam, 62, 94
Republicans, 41
Richard Young, 218

Roman Empire, 30
Saints, 113, 136, 163, 224
Same-sex marriage, 216, 245
Sanhedrin, 126, 127
Shammai, 15, 125, 126, 127, 128, 183, 249
Shem, 43
Socialist, 12, 13, 16, 17, 20
Society, 18, 158, 161, 256
Sodom and Gomorrah, 10, 242, 243
Sodomite, 225, 229
Solomon, 57, 58, 59, 60, 61, 62, 63, 65, 66, 68, 70, 71, 72, 73, 74, 75, 76, 77, 79, 80, 81, 83, 85, 86, 87, 88, 89, 90, 91, 92, 93, 94, 95, 96, 98, 99, 100, 101, 105, 248, 256,

257, 263
Straightway Baptist Church, 160
Talmud, 126, 249
Tamar, 119, 124
Temple Baptist Church, 150, 251
Tertullian, 178, 180, 181
Textus Receptus, 143, 154
The Bride, 51, 54, 57, 68, 85, 101
Thomas Aquinas, 185
Tirzah, 85, 86
Traditional, 240
Tribulation, 21
Unseemly, 223
Vaughn Walker, 217
W. Fisher-Hunter, 205, 252
Wisdom, 248, 257

ABOUT THE AUTHOR

Dr. Charles Kriessman has been saved since the Lord called him on September 12, 1983. He attends The Bible for Today Church in Collingswood, New Jersey, via Internet Streaming, since 2004. Pastor D.A. Waite, Th.D., Ph.D. is the Pastor of BFT.

Charles was born in Washington, D.C. sixty-four years ago. He has studied the subject of Bible Versions since 1985. He has written a book on the subject entitled, "Modern Version Failures."

He has attended Gustavus Adolphus College in St. Peter, Minnesota; Orange Coast College in Costa Mesa, California; and Macedonia Baptist College in Midland, North Carolina. Mr. Kriessman currently holds a doctorate in Biblical Studies from G.C.B.I. in Ft. Walton Beach, Florida.

www.ingramcontent.com/pod-product-compliance
Lightning Source LLC
Chambersburg PA
CBHW060500090426
42735CB00011B/2062